Policy and University Faculty Governance

Volume 4
Educational Policy in the 21st Century

Editors: Michael T. Miller and Julie Caplow
Series Editor: Bruce Anthony Jones

Policy and University Faculty Governance

Edited by
Michael T. Miller
University of Arkansas

Julie Caplow
University of Missouri–Columbia

INFORMATION AGE
PUBLISHING

80 Mason Street • Greenwich, Connecticut 06830 • www.infoagepub.com

Library of Congress Cataloging-in-Publication Data

Policy and university faculty governance / editors, Michael T.
    Miller and Julie Caplow.
       p. cm. — (Educational policy in the 21st century ; v. 4)
    Includes bibliographical references and index.
    ISBN 1-59311-073-1 — ISBN 1-59311-072-3 (pbk.)
    1. Universities and colleges—United States—Administration.
  2. Teacher participation in administration—United States.
  I. Miller, Michael T. II. Caplow, Julie. III. Series.
  LB2341.P617   2003
  378.1'1—dc21

                                 2003042915

Printed in the United States of America

CONTENTS

Part III.   Governance Issues and Trends

INTRODUCTION

This volume of the "Educational Policy in the 21st Century" series focuses on faculty governance in higher education. Faculty participation in decision making in colleges and universities represents a significant policy arena within the American educational system. Faculty have significant input into how policy is determined and implemented in colleges and universities because of their role in decisions regarding curriculum, student admission, and faculty employment, and their advisory role in budgetary matters. The concept of shared governance between faculty, administrators, and trustees is a unique aspect of higher education organizations. It is premised on the nature of academic work and influences the organizational structure and culture of American higher education.

As Vicki Rosser points out in the chapter, "Historical Overview of Faculty Governance in Higher Education," faculty participation in governance has evolved as the American higher education system has developed. The primary authority in the Colonial colleges rested with the boards of trustees of the colleges. As the nature of academic work became more specialized and complex, the governance pattern moved from authority vested in boards, to presidents, and to our current configuration of shared governance. Although boards of trustees carry the formalized authority for decisions regarding the functioning of academic organizations, that authority is delegated to faculty and administrators of the institution. The result of this is a system whereby faculty have primary authority for policy decisions regarding the major activities of the institutions and administration has primary authority for procedures for implementing those policies.

Policy and University Faculty Governance, vii–ix
Copyright © 2003 by Information Age Publishing

As colleges and universities are faced with pressures for increased accountability combined with fiscal restraints, faculty participation in policy formation and governance activities is becoming ever more important. Decisions regarding effective and efficient implementation of curricula, resource allocations, and admission criteria are critical for the functioning of higher education in the current environment.

Issues related to the role and functioning of the shared governance activities of faculty are explored in this volume. The volume is divided into three parts. The chapters in the first section explore the context in which the concept of shared governance has developed and is carried out. Vicki Rosser provides a historical overview of faculty governance in higher education. Kang Bai examines faculty involvement in governance from a national perspective. The final chapter of the section, by David Houston, contains a discussion of the role of state level coordinating and governing bodies, and the role of trustees in negotiating the interests of their individual institutions in this context. He maintains that trustees must balance the tensions between institution perspectives of autonomy and state perspectives of accountability.

The chapters in the second part of the volume focus on governance issues within an academic organization. Faculty have considerable influence into how policy is determined and implemented in colleges and universities. Michael Miller and Myron Pope present an overview of faculty governance roles within institutions, and the barriers and benefits to faculty participation in the major governance unit of colleges and universities; the faculty senate or council. A study of the participation and communication behaviors of faculty senate members is described in the chapter by Michael Miller, Carl Williams, and Brian Garavalia. The primary arena of faculty influence in decision making is at the departmental or academic unit level. Department chairs, as the "frontline" administrators are often caught in the middle of faculty and administrative interests, and are acutely aware of issues related to faculty governance, according to Steve Vacik in his chapter on the role of the chair. Vacik discusses how chairs play a critical role is framing how faculty participate in governance activities. The section concludes with a chapter by Kenneth Borland in which he explores the "We/They" relationship that can develop between faculty and administration in their shared governance endeavors. Faculty participation in decision making evolved in a collegial context in which administrators have come from the ranks of faculty at the institution and share with the faculty a common vision and purpose. Kenneth Borland points out that as the complexity of the higher education enterprise has grown, modern higher education administrators are more bureaucratic and political than their counterparts of the early and mid twentieth century. In addition, administrators often move from one institution to another, hence, may not share the vision of faculty at any one institution. The result of this can be increasing levels of mistrust between faculty and administrators. The authors of all the chapters in this section offer recommendations for improving faculty participation in governance and the relationship between faculty and administration as they carry out their shared governance functions.

The chapters in the final part of the volume, "Governance Issues and Trends," focus on different aspects of faculty governance. Ethan Heinen and Julie Caplow used an alternative investigative approach in an analysis of college novels, to explore the images that may be portrayed to the general public about faculty participation in decisions central to the operations of colleges and universities. The chapters in the first two parts focus primarily on the governance function of faculty in four-year colleges and universities. Myron Pope, in his chapter on faculty governance in community colleges, discusses the distinct perspective of two year colleges in the role of faculty in decision making. In discussion of faculty governance, the focus is typically on the major areas of faculty involvement in decisions; curriculum, faculty responsibilities and tenure, and admissions. Thomas Bila broadens this perspective with his discussion of the role of faculty in institutional fundraising.

This volume is intended to provide the reader with a broad view of the roles and responsibilities of faculty in organizational decision making in higher education, as well as, focused view of issues and trends related to faculty governance. Although the participation of faculty in policy formation in colleges and universities, through their participation in significant decisions affecting the functioning of the institution, is an established tradition, numerous trends may be impacting that role. Increased demands for accountability by the general public, and state and federal level policy makers; an increasingly bureaucratic, mobile, and political administration; and escalating demands on faculty to be entrepreneurial may influence faculty's levels of participation in governance activities. Careful analysis and examination of these trends coupled with an understanding of the traditional cogovernance roles of faculty and administration in higher education organizations is necessary for sound local and national policy formation.

Julie A. Caplow

PART I

THE CONTEXT

CHAPTER 1

HISTORICAL OVERVIEW OF FACULTY GOVERNANCE IN HIGHER EDUCATION

Vicki J. Rosser
University of Missouri–Columbia

The origins of faculty governance are deeply held traditions that continue to exist throughout higher education in the United States. The purpose of this chapter is to present a historical overview of the crucial time periods and important cases and issues that shaped faculty governance in contemporary higher education. This chapter will briefly trace the development of faculty governance in higher education from Europe to Colonial America, as well as provide an overview of faculty governance from the colonial period through the contemporary post-World War II era. In addition to these formative periods in higher education, important cases (e.g., Dartmouth, Yeshiva) and professional worklife issues (e.g., academic freedom, collective bargaining) which have influenced faculty members' participation in shared governance will also be examined.

Policy and University Faculty Governance, 3–17
Copyright © 2003 by Information Age Publishing

THE EUROPEAN UNIVERSITIES

Important traditions of faculty governance in higher education were firmly established as far back as twelth century Europe. These governance traditions evolved from the teaching guilds or student nations which were established in the regions of Northern and Southern Europe. The guilds or nations were voluntary associations of scholars and students who shared a common ethnic or regional identity and a common vernacular language. In the Southern European tradition of Bologna, Italy, universities were formed as students' *collegia* (Haskins, 1984). The student collegia were associations of foreign apprentice-scholars or guilds of students who wanted instruction. The guilds were initially formed as student nations for collective security and protection against the local authorities. Student nations, however, were also established to share in the university's academic life and decision making through their elected representatives in university assemblies, where actual governance occurred.

The students, in the Bologna tradition, retained control of the academic gathering place through their elected representatives. Students hired and fired the faculty, fixed their salaries, required each professor to swear allegiance and obedience to whatever statutes were enacted, granted leaves of absence, and controlled the smallest details of daily academic life (Lucas, 1994). The elected student representatives or *consiliarius* of the nations belonged to a university-wide senate presided over by a rector, who was elected by the members. The typical pattern was for the official rector to rotate among the various nations, so that all nations would be assured adequate representation of their respective interests. The primary purpose of the rector was to exercise both civil and criminal jurisdiction over students and professors. In 1158 the German Emperor Barbarossa granted a charter that provided special protected rights and privileges to the local *studia* in Bologna from the local authorities (e.g., church and state).

In contrast, the Northern European tradition of Paris, France, guilds of faculty members came together and formed a university or institution. Renowned faculty[1] members from specialized disciplines began to attract large numbers of students. These gatherings provided an organizing place for students and faculty to be drawn together by a common interest in learning. During this formative period, almost any academic gathering was commonly referred to as a studium ("place of study"), which had evolved from the earlier cathedral school of Paris (Rudy, 1984). Collective meetings of the universitas or studium were conducted weekly and proceedings of the University Assembly resembled meetings of the faculty nations as a body. Corresponding to the executive council (or University Assembly) of the faculty was a general University Council, consisting of the deans of faculties of law, medicine, and theology, the proctor of the arts faculty, and an elected chief rector who served as head of the university as a whole, including its so-called higher faculties (Rudolph, 1962).

In the early 1200s, there was a conflict between local religious authorities and Parisian Master's (faculty) over the university's right to control the licensing of teachers. Traditionally, licensure had been the sole and exclusive prerogative of the Church; ecclesiastical officials opposed the master's guilds when they began insisting on the right to establish their own rules for the admission of new members (Haskins, 1984). The teaching master's established rules governing the qualifications of those who would be allowed to teach. The Church moved to counter the growing power of the masters' guilds, which they regarded as a direct threat to their own authority. Confrontations ensued, and finally, in 1215 Pope Innocent III suggested a compromise that in effect legitimized the guilds' right to set licensing standards, though reserving the actual right of bestowal to chancellors or other high cathedral officials (Lucas, 1994). Similar to the Bologna chapter, the Parisian Master's also received special status from the church. The Pope reaffirmed the authority of the faculty over the university. The faculties embraced the *papal bull* because the pope's edict confirmed their control over the conditions which licensure for teachers was granted.

Attaining special status from the church allowed or established the faculty right to determine *who would teach* and *what would be taught*. Thus, faculty members' autonomy and shared governance were established very early on in the history of higher education. Bologna was granted the right to establish its own teaching qualifications in 1291; Paris had the same privilege conferred by Nicholas IV in 1292, and it is these rights and privileges that became the common pattern in most of the medieval universities established thereafter. The words, *"who shall teach and what shall be taught,"* are referred to as the most important rights and privileges won by the university (Lucas, 1994). Over a half century later, little question remains that a full fledged university was then firmly established.

Despite conflict, by the late 1400s new universities appeared throughout Europe. Whether universities were governed by faculty members or students, both types of academic institutions proliferated throughout Europe at an increasing rate between the thirteenth and fifteenth centuries (Rudy, 1984). University proliferation, however, did not occur without conflict from the local authorities. Hearing of the local turmoil in Paris, the English King, Henry III, sought to take advantage of the situation by extending an invitation to the scholars of the Northen tradition of faculty guilds to transfer to the kingdom of England. Two institutions, Oxford and Cambridge, were established as a result of the Parisian riots and conflicts. Many of the scholars and students who came to Oxford were fleeing the scorn and heavy hand of church and state. From Paris, these scholars and students brought with them their academic customs, titles, and ceremonies. Internal difficulties at Oxford later gave rise to another mass exodus of scholars who founded another university, Cambridge. Major conflicts ensued between "town and gown" (local authorities and faculty guilds), primarily over prices in ale, food, and rent.

Where local turmoil existed, the king did not take the side of business or other authorities' interests in disputes. Rather, the king granted these universities independence, and they were considered to have autonomy. The great medieval universities were established, and they emerged as independent institutions with power and prestige by virtue of king and church tradition (Rudolph, 1962). Again, the 1300s firmly established the corporate authority of *who teaches and what is taught*, which means that the university was protected from outside control. Faculties enjoyed the unchallenged authority, and control over learning and scholarship were respected and abided. Faculty members actually managed the institution's operational affairs, despite their struggle for autonomy and independent control. Throughout the medieval times in Europe, the greatest threats to academic freedom came from the encroachments of church or state through the depredations of popes, secular monarchs, and local civil authorities (Lucas, 1994). In essence, corporate authority or institutional autonomy was reflective of the medieval construction of academic freedom. By the sixteenth and seventeenth centuries, English colleges were semiautonomous corporations, and each was headed by a principal elected by peers to administer the college's affairs. As a center of learning where learning was advanced, preserved, stimulated, and codified, the university served as an oasis of intellectual freedom in an age profoundly suspicious of the slightest taint of heresy (Lucas, 1994).

THE COLONIAL PERIOD

The establishment of the American colonial colleges mirrored the Oxford and Cambridge models influenced by king and church. As higher education moved to the colonies there were three differences that existed between the American and the British or European models: (1) the influence of church and the mission of college were intertwined (private denominational sponsorship); (2) the autonomy of the faculty was not immediately established, because the American colleges started with a president, and the president initially taught; and (3) the establishment of a layboard or governing board that was not part of the institution, or did not include part of the faculty (or president), but an external overseeing body that did not exist in the European model.

As the rising tide of religious influence engulfed America's colonial colleges in the eighteenth century, traditional patterns of faculty governance between church and state were being challenged. At that time, higher education lost much of its original purpose and function in the European tradition. Sectarian passions contributed to the founding of any given college, and the custodians of these colleges never lost sight of their larger religious purpose (Rudolph, 1990). Religious diversity, however, throughout the colonies prevented any one sect or denomination to exercise exclusive control over the college that was established. No college found it possible to impose a religious test for admission or doctrinal requirements for graduation, and members of minority congregations invariably were assured freedom of religious belief while attending a particular school of dominant faith (Brubacher & Rudy, 1968; Lucas, 1994). The religious and sectarian influence in these first American institutions was felt in a number of colonial colleges.

Harvard, as the first American colonial college established by clergy, was chartered in 1636 as the first bicameral form of college and administration with two boards (Brubacher & Rudy, 1968): (1) the external lay body or overseers, which represented the founders, and (2) the corporate internal board of the English tradition, with the president and fellows or faculty members. The external body (or board) oversaw policy formulation and the allocation of financial resources. The internal corporate board handled the discipline of students and directed curriculum and instruction. The corporate board consisting of the faculty and the president was subject to the overseers composed primarily of magistrates and clergy. The English Crown, therefore, delegated the power to the Harvard board to perform the functions and mission of the college. Essentially, the Harvard overseers were the university, and they were given corporate authority and power. By the end of the seventeenth century, Harvard faculty members tried to curtail the power of the overseers, but failed when the English Crown rejected their request to change the charter's status. Although the change in the charter's status was rejected, in 1826 the overseers published a new set of statutes that allowed for the creation of a bicameral system of institutional governance.

In 1693, William and Mary was established with a similar structure, but kept the European tradition of a self-governing faculty more clearly defined. The president at William and Mary was considered a *first among equals* on a faculty of resident masters who comprised the corporation (Rudolph, 1990). Faculty autonomy, however, was eclipsed by a board of trustees wherein authority was divided between a body consisting of trustees and another of a faculty (Brubacher & Rudy, 1968). Initially, the trustees were empowered to appoint presidents and legislate for the college, but the charter directed that ultimately they were to surrender these powers and the property of the college to the faculty. It was not until 1729 that the trustees, with much hesitation, carried out this aspect of the founding charter. Thereafter, the trustees receded into the background as a board of visitors, and the faculty became as nearly self-governing in the traditional sense as any American college (Young, 1949).

In 1701, Yale was founded and governed during the colonial period by a board comprised of ten disgruntled Harvard clergy. The Connecticut Legislature granted the institution's charter to the ten clergymen or trustees as a legal corporation. This legislative move established that the board of trustees hold the charter for the institution, which was deemed the institution, and therefore, the institution would not legally exist without the charter. Essentially, the state legislature handed the charter in trust to the institution's board of trustees. The board of trustees were then entrusted with the college's past, present, and future. Boards of trustees were established with two primary responsibilities: (1) to protect the financial interests of the institution—to sustain itself, and to protect the charter and; (2) to choose or dismiss the president. The function of the Yale board as a single absentee or nonresident body of clergymen inaugurated a type of governing board that would become the American standard for higher education (Rudolph, 1990). The development of nonresident control or external lay boards changed the president from being either first among equals or leader of the faculty into something far different—a representative of the governing board and a significant power in his own right (Kirkpatrick, 1931, as cited in Rudolph, 1962; Hofstadter & Metzger, 1955). In 1748, Princeton added the governor of New Jersey and four members of the governor's council to their board of trustees. In this case, the unique governance structure was established a means to prevent religious intrusion, rather than to establish significant ties with the state (Wertenbaker, 1946).

THE ANTEBELLUEM PERIOD

After the American revolution, institutions of higher education were no longer chartered by the English Crown; the colonies were chartering their own institutions. States were given the land through land grants; states had the land, and state governments had the charter to begin an institution. In turn, the state put the charter in the hands of the board and the board was to oversee the institution. Once the charter was given to the board, issues between board and state ensued over how much autonomy should be given to the institution's board versus how much control the state will retain. The delicate relationship among state, board, and institution continued for some time until the Dartmouth case of 1769 established institutional independence in American higher education.

The College of Dartmouth was originally established by royal charter from the English Crown, and the charter was given to the institution's self-perpetuating board. Dartmouth's president, Elezar Wheelock died and his son John Wheelock took over as President. Shortly thereafter, conflicts between John Wheelock and the board intensified and he was asked to resign by the board. The Wheelock family appealed to the New Hampshire state government. The state government reorganized the school as a state university, reorganized the board, and reinstated John Wheelock as president. The case was then appealed to the state supreme court who ruled that the college charter, given by the English Crown, was not to be altered by the state, reaffirming that the original charter of the institution stays with the board.

The Dartmouth Case had established two precedents in American higher education. First, that private institutions will remain under private control. This landmark case ensured the difference between private and public institutions. The case also established that only through financial exigency, (that is, the private school or college is unable to function), and the state wants to take control, can the state then take control of the institution. Second, that institutional independence was solidified for privates. College independence from state control began to spread to public institutions, because in some cases the charter was still held by the board, which resulted in institutional independence from state government, and the state government could not interfere with the private control of institutions. The Dartmouth Case provided effective barriers against the external forces (e.g., state) pressing for control of higher education.

Faculty governance in the antebellum college typically existed as a matter of *one-man rule*, usually paternalistic, and sometimes autocratic (Lucas, 1994). During the early nineteenth century, the president (rector, provost, chancellor, principal) was in charge, and *he* was answerable only to an external or nonresident board of trustees or governors. Although faculty members (tutors) did not easily submit to the autocratic rule of a strong president, they served at the president's pleasure and could very well be dismissed at will. Moreover, faculty members did not readily acquiesce to the authority of political appointees, clergymen, or wealthy benefactors as trustees whose claims to academic legitimacy they often questioned (Brubacher & Rudy, 1968). Despite the onset of power struggles between faculty and administration, when a president was directly threatened by the faculty of the institution, usually the president could depend on the college's governors for backing. In those colleges where faculty governance remained strong, there were limits to presidential authority and power. In the majority of cases, however, there was little to prevent a strong-willed executive officer from ruling with an iron hand. Increasingly, a president's position was strengthened by a growing acceptance that college administrators and academics were two different breeds entirely (Rudolph, 1990). The compromise that proved most enduring was to allow decisions regarding student admissions, academic standards, and curriculum to be controlled by faculty, while in all other matters the board and the president most often held sway (Lucas, 1994).

THE POST-CIVIL WAR PERIOD

American faculty members who were schooled in the traditions of academe were a closely-knit, somewhat insular community of scholars. In the late 1800s and early 1900s, faculty members within colleges began to view the administration as more of a corporate body. The administration valued orderliness, efficiency, and accountability, and the new hand of the business oriented president was beginning to control every aspect of the modern university (Brubacher & Rudy, 1968). These were the first signs of a faculty that began to worry about their place within the power structure of the academic organization. In contrast to origins in Europe, there existed rudiments of faculty consultation and participation in governance; however, little amounted to more than a symbolic gesture extended by the president and board who held the real power (Lucas, 1994). The issue was whether faculty members, individually or collectively, exercised any substantial control over the circumstances of their own work.

In 1876, more than 200 years after the establishment of Harvard with the president running the institution, Johns Hopkins was established as the first American research university under the German model of governance. For the first time in American higher education, graduate education (i.e., master's, doctorate) was emphasized, and as a result, more emphasis was placed on the faculty. Graduate education required a new and advanced curriculum with more specialization beyond the general core curriculum, and curriculum specialization required more faculty members, and more faculty members lead to increased power for the faculty.

Especially impressive to American scholars was the Germanic emphasis on the pursuit of truth through original scholarly investigation (academic freedom). The German academic traditions were based on two fundamental ideas. The first, *Lernfreiheit*, or "freedom to learn," meant university students were allowed to choose whatever courses they preferred, with no formal attendance requirements or tests whatsoever, preliminary to their applying for a final degree examination (Lucas, 1994; Rudolph, 1990). The second, *Lehrfreiheit*, or "freedom to teach," signified the scholar's right to pursue investigation wherever it might lead, to draw from research whatever conclusions were warranted, and to disseminate the results through teaching or publication without hindrance or interference from external authorities (Lucas, 1994; Rudolph, 1990). These two traditions were perceived as an absolute right and considered sacrosanct in the German model. If corporate interests or agents were allowed to dictate what a professor might teach, the integrity of all scholarship within a college or university was directly threatened (Veysey, 1965). Only in the university could there emerge the dual traditions of *Lernfreiheit* and *Lehrfreiheit* essential to its academic mission. The rise of the American research university effectively ended the religious influence on teaching and learning (Haskins, 1957).

As a result of the research university and faculty disciplinary specialization, the academic department was established and became key to the faculty's power and authority in decision making and institutional governance. The faculty reside in the department and much of their power also resides at the department level; faculty members were less accountable to higher authorities (e.g., president, board). Decision making at the department level is the most autonomous and collegial, and it is within departments that faculty members make their most significant decisions and contributions to institutional governance (Baldridge, 1971).

Areas under the purview of faculty members are course and curricular content, assignment of faculty members to teaching and research, standards for admissions to programs, graduation and degree requirements, academic policy, and academic advising. Although departments foster disciplinary specialization, departments must also be interdependent with other units within the college or institution (e.g., PhD requirements work in conjunction with other PhD programs). Thus, in the 1890s, a hierarchical arrangement emerged, long familiar in business though new to academia, which roughly paralleled the administrative rankings: department heads, full professors, associate and assistant professors, instructors, and several classes of graduate students (Veysey, 1965). At the top of the institutional structure remained the board of trustees and the president.

ACADEMIC FREEDOM

Job security had always been a tenuous affair among the nineteenth century American professoriat (Lucas, 1994; Rudolph, 1990; Veysey, 1965). Previously, job security was threatened by taking a stand contrary to prevailing religious orthodoxy. At the end of the nineteenth century, however, the grounds shifted to the political and economic arenas. Often, the faculty member publicly urged reforms or criticized the existing social order, and was then summarily dismissed for causing trouble (Lucas, 1994). Coupled with professors' demands for academic freedom was a plea for greater job security. From a faculty perspective, academe should be a protected place, and since the colonial times anything much resembling academic freedom in its modern sense was either nonexistent or severely limited. Consequently, the demand for the freedom to teach and publish without fear of hindrance were virtually impossible to achieve.

The principles of academic freedom and tenure were established during a time when faculty members were acutely aware of the disjunction between society and its institutions (Rudolph, 1962, 1990). Conflicts with businessmen ensued, and out of these experiences developed important standards of freedom and tenure affecting the capacity of the American university to support effectively the life of the mind (Fuess, 1935). Each case became the right of the professor to the same freedom of expression enjoyed by businessmen, farmers, and workers (Rudolph, 1962, 1990). In addition to the principles of academic freedom was the establishment of academic tenure. Academics argued for greater job security, rank and seniority, and salary schedules.

The establishment of tenure provided a means for managing permanent and temporary appointments, expectations of working conditions conducive to scholarly work, and collective commitment to the principles of academic freedom (Lucas, 1994). By the 1900s faculty members were being professionalized, and institutional boards were being pressured to recognize their obligations to the community of free scholars (Hofstadter & Metzger, 1955; Rogers, 1942). As a profession, therefore, faculty members have an obligation to censure themselves, provide ethical standards, and implement fair mechanisms for peer review and hiring within their academic communities. In essence, faculty members have the authority and the responsibility to pass judgment on themselves.

In 1915 the American Association for University Professors (AAUP) was established as a means to protect academic freedom. The AAUP was established as a professional society dedicated to the development and protection of standards of academic freedom and tenure (Rudolph, 1990). The birth of the AAUP was bolstered by a need to defend academic freedom and to bolster tenure and procedural safeguards against arbitrary dismissal of errant faculty members (Lucas, 1994; Metzger, 1955). The AAUP prepared a draft Statement of Principles outlining the importance of safeguarding academic freedom and tenure in the nation's colleges and universities. The AAUP became the single most influential and important defender of professorial tenure and academic freedom (AAUP, 1965, pp. 110, 116-117). The intent was that professors should reclaim their rightful role in the governance of colleges and universities. Academic freedom to determine *who shall teach* and *what shall be taught and published* was well established before the early 1800s.

COLLECTIVE BARGAINING

Another important development in the history of faculty governance was the right for faculty to collectively bargain. The next important time period for faculty governance occurred in 1965 when the states of Michigan and New York allowed public employees to organize and bargain collectively. In 1951, however, the National Labor Relations Board (NLRB) had decided to exclude college and university employees from the right to collectively bargain. This refusal to assert jurisdiction remained in force until 1970, when the NLRB reversed themselves and allowed the National Labor Relations Act (NLRA) to apply to faculty members as well.

Then in 1975, Yeshiva University (a private institution) appealed the right of full time faculty members to collectively bargain and organize. The institution argued that faculty members were managerial employees, because they had a role in the governance and decision making of the institution, and they should not be required to negotiate with their own management (Olivas, 1989). The administrative perspective was that faculty members want to run the institution, but act like labor to negotiate salary and working conditions. On the other hand, the faculty argued that they wanted a hand in governance, but the administration had the dominant influence. For example, the administration controls the budget via academic policy, yet administrators do not participate in governance mechanisms such as faculty councils. The appeal was upheld. The Yeshiva Case (1980) went on to the U.S. Court of Appeals, and the decision was affirmed by the Supreme Court. The controlling consideration in this case was that faculty members of Yeshiva University exercise authority which in any other context unquestionably would be managerial. As a result of the Yeshiva Case, almost 60 private institutions dropped their cases to organize, and the shift for institutions to collectively bargain with faculty members on Yeshiva-grounds immediately stopped (Olivas, 1989).

Since the first college faculties were unionized in the 1960s and 1970s, collective bargaining had become widespread in higher education (Olivas, 1989). By 1984, 830 of the 3,284 institutions in the United States were covered by faculty collective bargaining agreements (Douglas, 1988). The majority of institutions were public (83%), and bargaining did not hit the private institutions as to the same extent. Most collective bargaining occurred at the community colleges, and occurred least at research universities. The Yeshiva decision, in part, encouraged a more collegial view of faculty members' participation in governance. Universities, such as Yeshiva, depend on faculty members' professional judgement and expertise to formulate policies that meet institutional goals.

CONTEMPORY FACULTY GOVERNANCE

Governance in contemporary higher education in the United States is most often defined as the structure and process for college and university decision making at the institutional, systemwide, or state level (Mortimer & McConnell, 1991). One of the most common forms of decision making in higher education is *shared governance*—the sharing of authority by the various constituent or stakeholder groups in making those decisions (Berdahl, 1991). There are several different levels of governance in higher education in which both internal and external sets of constituents affect or influence the process of institutional decision making. For example, public institutions are usually overseen by statewide or systemwide governing boards, with members appointed by the state's governor. The most typical structure of governance, in both public and private institutions, is a board of trustees at the institutional level empowered to make a wide range of decisions concerning the institution in their care. In the majority of higher education institutions in the United States, there also exists some form of internal governance that encompasses a complex distribution of decision making shared by the faculty, administration, and in many cases students.

There are three arenas within an institution's system of governance in which faculty are called on to formulate their views in the decision-making process. One arena of decision making resides within the faculty members' department in a particular discipline or disciplines. In the academic department, the content of individual courses, the substance of research, the methods of instruction, and decisions on faculty hiring, promotion, retirement, and dismissal of members are determined by the faculty. A second arena includes faculty committees, standing committees on academic affairs and financial affairs, or other committees created to formulate opinions on particular problems or issues as they arise. For example, faculty views regarding student diversity, admissions policies, and the allocation of resources proposed in the annual budget are usually shaped and expressed through committee work.

And third, most colleges and universities have a campus-wide deliberative body such as a faculty senate or council that plays a major role in shaping formal recommendations on most academic matters (e.g., curriculum, faculty tenure/promotion status, program and degree requirements, professional activities, and student performance). The senate is the mechanism through which recommendations are formulated by a representative body of the faculty. Thus, the faculty as a deliberative body has the responsibility to debate matters of academic concern, to voice their findings, and to have them heard. In the case where faculty senates and unions coexist in colleges and universities, there generally appears to be a division of responsibilities (Birnbaum, 1991). Faculty senates tend to exert their greatest power and influence over academic matters and unions have traditionally focused on economic issues such as salaries, working conditions, and job security. Joint responsibility between unions and faculty senates tend to cover personnel issues such as hiring, promotion, and tenure. The extent to which faculty members participate in the decision-making process through these three areas of governance (i.e., departments, committees, faculty senates) varies from institution to institution, and of course, the aggressiveness of the faculty. Historically, the degree of faculty influence may also vary by institutional control (i.e., public vs. private) and the amount of authority designated by the institution's president or board of trustees (Baldridge, Curtis, Ecker, & Riley, 1991).

CONCLUSION

The degree of institutional autonomy and faculty members' right to determine *who shall teach and what shall be taught and published* are deeply held academic traditions within the history of governance in higher education. To fully understand the importance of faculty governance as it exists today, there must be an appreciation of the historical context in which these traditions were firmly established. In the past, the greatest threat to the academy derived from the powerful influence of church and state. In contemporary higher education, however, threats to faculty members' role in governance and to their professional work would seem to come from a variety of external influences, market forces, and the globalization of the political economy (Slaughter & Leslie, 1997). Therefore, it is important to value the fundamental tenets in the development of faculty governance in higher education, and to appreciate those faculty members and students who built the foundation of academic governance by seeking out a place to study, to learn, and to teach.

NOTE

1.   Those scholars who studied and taught in a particular field or subject came to be referred to as a "faculty," a term derived from the medieval Latin *facultas*, meaning a strength or power to do a specific thing, and therefore, an

appropriate designation for the various subject-matter divisions of the teacher's guild (Elliott, 1968).

REFERENCES

American Association for University Professors. (1965, May). Report of a self-survey committee on the American association of university professors. *American Association of University Professors Bulletin, 51*, 110, 116-117.

Baldridge, J. V. (1971). *Academic governance.* Berkeley, CA: McCutchan.

Baldridge, J. V., Curtis, D. V., Ecker, G., & Riley, G. L. (1991). Alternative models of governance in higher education. In M. Peterson (Ed.), *Organization and governance in higher education* (4th ed., pp. 30-45). Needham Heights, MA: Simon & Schuster.

Berdahl, R. O. (1991). Shared governance and external constraints. In M. Peterson (Ed.), *Organization and governance in higher education* (4th ed., pp. 217-224). Needham Heights, MA: Simon & Schuster.

Birnbaum, R. (Ed.). (1991). The latent organizational functions of the academic senate: Why senates do not work but will not go away. *New Directions for Higher Education, Faculty Governance (No. 75, The Role of Senates and Joint Committees in Academic Decision Making), 19*(3), 7-25.

Brubacher, J. S., & Rudy, E. (1968). *Higher education in transition.* New York: Harper & Row.

Douglas, J. (1988). Professors on strike: An analysis of two decades of faculty work stoppages, 1966-85. *The Labor Lawyer, 4*, 87-101.

Elliott, J. H. (1968). *Europe divided, 1559-1598.* New York: Harper & Row.

Fuess, C. M. (1935). *Amherst: The story of a New England college.* Boston: Little Brown and Co.

Haskins, C. H. (1984). *The rise of universities.* New York: Cornell University Press.

Hofstadter, R., & Metzger, W. P. (1955). *The development of academic freedom in the United States.* New York: Columbia University Press.

Lucas, C. J. (1994). *American higher education: A history.* New York: St. Martin's Griffin.

Metzger, W. P. (1955). *Academic freedom: In the age of the university.* New York: Columbia University Press.

Mortimer, K. P., & McConnell, T. R. (1991). Process of academic governance. In M. Petersen (Ed.), *Organization and governance in higher education* (4th ed., pp. 164-174). Needham Heights: Simon & Schuster.

Olivas, M. A. (1989). *The law and higher education: Cases and materials on colleges in court.* Durham, NC: Carolina Academic Press.

Rogers, W. P. (1942). *Andrew D. White and the modern university.* Ithaca, NY: Cornell University.

Rudolph, F. (1962). *The American college and university: A history.* New York: Random House.

Rudolph, F. (1990). *The American college and university: A history.* Athens, GA: The University of Georgia Press.

Rudy, W. (1984). *The universities of Europe, 1100-1914*. Cranbury, NJ: Associated University Presses.

Slaughter, S., & Leslie, L. L. (1997). *Academic capitalism: Politics, policies, and the entrepreneurial university*. Baltimore: Johns Hopkins University Press.

Veysey, L. R. (1965). *The emergence of the American university*. Chicago, IL: The University of Chicago Press.

Wertenbaker, T. J. (1946). *Princeton 1746-1896*. Princeton, NJ: Princeton University Press.

Young, B. B. (1949, October). What is a college? *Educational Record, 30*(4), 385-406.

CHAPTER 2

THE NATIONAL SCENE

Faculty Involvement in Governance

Kang Bai
Troy State University Dothan

Faculty involvement in governance has been an important part of college and university administration in U.S. higher education. Although the practice has not yet found a general understanding among college administrators or even faculty themselves, faculty involvement in governance is gaining in momentum and drawing more and more attention from college administrators and scholars or experts in higher education administration. According to Gilmour (1991), approximately 90% of all colleges and universities in America today involve faculty in governance activities. In addition, community colleges, as addressed by Pope and Miller (1999), are increasingly called on to provide faculty members with opportunities for broad-based participation in decision making that affects both colleges operations and policies. In this process faculty play a crucial role in the institutional decision making with regard to instruction, curriculum, budgeting, and policy formation. Miller (1997) described the faculty involvement in governance as vital to institutional success and related to more positive attitudes toward teaching and institutional affinity.

The purpose of this chapter is to present a general picture of the faculty involvement in governance in colleges and universities throughout

Policy and University Faculty Governance, 19–30

the country. Issues related to faculty governance will be discussed, barriers to faculty participation will be brought up, and approaches and skills for involving more faculty members in the governance process will be reviewed as suggestions and recommendations.

The concept that best reflects the ways in which college and universities differ from other organizations is governance (Birnbaum, 1988). Although there is no single and generally accepted definition, governance is in essence a matter of decision making, or a governing system that addresses the primary responsibility for an institution, or put in a direct way, refers to us "Who is in charge in the institution?"

In its more than 300 years of history, American higher education has experienced three major changes in governance. According to Birnbaum (1988) and Keller (1989), in the earliest times, when institutions were small and religious, boards of trustees, mostly clergymen, exercised the full authority and dominated everything on campus. In the late nineteenth century, the originally tiny, religious schools were changed to large state or private colleges and universities, and with the change, presidents took over and became the absolute authority on campuses. In the middle 1920s, with the founding of the American Association of University Professors (AAUP), faculty on many campuses began getting involved in governance, but at a slow, constrained, and cautious pace, and mostly in matters of curriculum and academic personnel. The late 1980s, however, witnessed a turning point in the history of academic participation in the direction of colleges and universities, when faculty started playing a positive and significant role in shared governance and got actively involved in deciding campus matters.

One of the typical features when faculty got seriously involved, as was pointed out by Keller (1989), was that top university administrators and leading faculty were combining their efforts in a new kind of cabinet government that advised on the priorities for action, educational focus, and expenditures for institutions. At the same time, academic governance and management began trying new patterns and experimenting with novel kinds of campus decision making. Ever since then college faculty have had a vital role in the determination of curricula, methods of instruction, policy of admission and graduation, selection and evaluation of faculty, and budget allocation on most of the campuses.

SHARED GOVERNANCE

Shared governance, as defined by Eckel (2000), is a system composed of structures and processes, through which faculty, administrators, and other campus constituents make collective institutional decisions. Early in 1984, the AAUP published an important and influential normative statement on governance, the "Joint Statement on Government of Colleges and Universities," articulating the concept of governance as a shared responsibility and joint effort involving all important constituents of the academic community (Birnbaum, 1988). Eckel (2000) noted that because not all decisions fall neatly into the domain of one of the three groups (faculty, administrators, and trustees), much of the institutional governance was and should be conducted jointly. Accordingly, up till now, shared governance is a commonly practiced governance system on most of the campuses. The past few decades of practice and experiences have shown that, though much more work still needs to be done, shared governance is an ideal form of governance in higher education and it actually answers the previous question: Who is in charge in the institution.

The American higher education system is the envy of the world. Every year it brings in tens of thousands of foreign students from other countries, adding to the already large student population from within the United States. At the same time, however, many colleges and universities are working hard to respond to the changing environments and experiencing difficulties that arise with the changes. Paradoxically, while the American colleges and universities are highly effective and successful, difficulties and problems exist. Because of that, many believe the college management and administration is problematic, colleges and universities are poorly run, and all those difficulties are due to governance, thus laying bare the issue of college governance and bringing forth the necessity of an innovative and efficient governance system to match the management and performance of colleges and universities so that even greater effectiveness and success will be achieved.

The issue of governance has concerned the roles of trustees, administrators, and faculty. Although the 1966 Statement on Governance of Colleges and Universities had outlined the roles for faculty, administrators, and trustees in governance decision, suggesting, for instance, that issues such as managing endowment be assigned to trustees, maintaining and creating new resources to the presidents, and developing the curriculum to the faculty (Eckel, 2000), problems still remain unsolved. Boards of trustees, increasingly made up of businessmen (approximately 40% or over), usually focus their interest on efficiency and do not understand the unique nature of the academic enterprise; they are likely to understand inadequately and support less the principles of academic freedom, and tend to believe more that certain academic decisions do not require faculty involvement (Birnbaum, 1988). As a matter of fact, however, the shifts in governance as mentioned above have left the board of trustees with little authority over the (major) function of the university, instruction

(Besse, 1973, as cited in Birnbaum, 1988), although calls for greater trustee involvement in governance have been increasing in recent years.

On the other hand, the focus of recent discussions has mostly been directed on the shared responsibilities between administrators and faculty. Colleges and universities were not established for administration but for teaching and learning. While the heart of a college beats in the classrooms, laboratories, and libraries, where faculty play a key role, the administrative role is ... to serve (faculty) as their assistants and cater to their idiosyncratic needs (Birnbaum, 1988), giving support and help to the faculty, creating a climate appropriate for completing teaching tasks, and ensuring the accomplishment of the missions and goals of the institution. Birnbaum further pointed out that to the extent that this was not done, the university would lose effectiveness. This clearly states the relationships between faculty and administrators as well as the importance of faculty role in the management and administration process.

Because of the direct involvement in teaching and learning, faculty are familiar with instruction, curricula, qualifications for teaching personnel, and requirements for admissions and graduation. In addition, due to their direct contact with the students in the process of teaching and learning, faculty understand the needs on the part of the students and know the best ways to help them grow academically, professionally, and ethically. Therefore, it is wise to involve faculty and give them the best say in the decision-making process relating to areas of academic affairs as well as areas affecting student lives and their academic development. In matters of academe and educational policies, faculty members are the experts who have the knowledge and expertise and should have the principle voice in decision making. Without faculty's participation, support, and acceptance, any attempts to make institutional changes would fail, no changes would have significant impact, nor could a university be successful.

In contemporary colleges and universities, however, many more areas of specialized knowledge and expertise are required to accomplish institutional missions, goals, and other administrative tasks. Such areas may include legal precedents, federal regulations, management information system, student financial aid procedures, and so forth, that require special skills, training, and capacities in management and administration and need individuals with specific qualifications not only to do the tasks but also to do the tasks well. Taking that into consideration, the process of management and administration can become so complex that even those faculty who are interested in governance may not have the time or the expertise to fully understand the processes of decision making or resource acquisition and allocation that are at the heart of many governance issues (Birnbaum, 1988). Something must be done to combine the efforts and expertise of both faculty and administrators in the process of decision making and those decisions which do not fall into the domain of only faculty, administrators, or trustees, such as those concerning general education policy, the framing and execution of strategic plans, budgeting, and presidential selection, should be made jointly. Therefore, while faculty and administrators, with different backgrounds and expertise, each fill different roles and fulfill specific tasks, a combination of faculty and administrators, and other related constituents, will be a best and ideal governance model, or a system of shared governance.

FACULTY ROLE EXPECTATIONS AND
RESPONSIBILITIES IN GOVERNANCE

The shared governance process requires the participation of both faculty and administrators. Faculty involvement, as a common practice in most institutions, usually presents itself in the forms of faculty senates or councils, which Miller et al. (1996) identified as an ideal mechanism for gaining faculty involvement or participation. In addressing the necessity of a faculty senate or council, Weingartner (1996) pointed out that the participation of a senate could help shape positions that pertained to the entire institution and conferred on them a legitimacy that was relevant both to the members of the institution and to the world outside it. Therefore, a faculty senate or council could always speak for the whole institution in peaceful times or in times of crisis, especially at times when administrators acting on their own were inadequate as spokesperson for the policies and interests of the institutions.

On the other hand, faculty's roles in governance can often be seen on many campuses focusing on areas of instruction, curriculum, requirements for admissions and graduation, teaching personnel, and so forth. On some campuses faculty also play a part in such areas as budgeting review, educational policy changes, and institutional renovation. In addition, Miller et al. (1996) found that the roles of faculty in decision making included involvement in developing specific outcomes for budgetary expenditure, clarifying administrator roles, and insisting on appropriate rights and responsibilities for faculty in governance In 2000, Eckel conducted a study of the faculty governance. In his study, the roles of the faculty in shared governance process were further justified in institutional hard decision-making process.

Hard decisions, such as decisions on continuance or discontinuance of an academic program, can be both hard and difficult "as the outcomes can be emotionally charged (Dill & Sporn, 1995, as cited in Eckel, 2000), faculty may lose their jobs and have their life's work interrupted (American Association of University Professors, 1995, as cited in Eckel, 2000), and the cuts can potentially threaten institutions' core values and alter institutional identities (Melchiori, 1982, as cited in Eckel, 2000). Yet the successful roles of faculty in making this kind of decision can best substantiate the value of faculty to the institution. Eckel's findings suggested that the responsibility for creating good shared governance was itself shared between faculty and administrators who could work together to get the job done when hard decisions needed to be made. In his study he found both faculty and administrators had active and positive attitudes toward the hard decision making, in the process of which faculty were mainly responsible for making institutional issues a priority and administrators were responsible for creating the climate in which good governance could operate. Through his study, he refuted the belief that more authority for administrators would lead to better institutional decision making and emphasized the importance of faculty's role in the share governance by pointing out that "where administrators do not frame the challenges in ways meaningful to faculty, ... do not draw upon legitimate avenues of faculty involvement, and do not tap faculty strengths such as exploring implications and acting as systems of checks and balance, shared governance cannot be expected to work well."

Now more and more administrators and faculty have come to see the roles of faculty as critical to the success of an institution. Specifically, administrators and faculty on most of the campuses have realized that any neglect of the encouragement and support of faculty leadership in institutional decision-making process may lead to eventual serious damages on any campuses and administrators who defer maintenance of faculty roles in governance are actually placing their institutions in a danger zone (Plante, 1989).

BARRIERS TO FACULTY INVOLVEMENT IN GOVERNANCE

Since faculty started getting involved in governance over 80 years ago, there have been misconceptions about and objections to faculty involvement in the process of the institutional decision making. Some misconceptions and objection come from the public who do not understand well the structures and processes of a university, some come from administrators who separate themselves from the faculty because of distrust, and others come from faculty themselves, who feel that their primary responsibility is to their discipline and students and they should serve them by concentrating on teaching and scholarship. Miller et al. (1996) addressed the barriers as presented by statewide coordinating boards to distrust of faculty and administrators towards each other. Furthermore, Miller (1997) summarized the barriers to involving faculty in institutional decision making, which included trust between faculty and administrators, no compensation for increased commitment and work production, faculty burnout due to overwork load, insufficient time for faculty to participate, and lack of abilities to work in unfamiliar areas. Among the many barriers, the following are worth our attention:

1. **Public Misconceptions:** The misunderstanding of faculty involvement in governance on the part of the public usually comes from lack of knowledge of the workings of the higher education system. Regarding faculty governance in colleges and universities, some ideas and opinions have but negative impacts on the public opinions that affect faculty participation in the governance process. Some critics of faculty governance thought that faculty should not be involved in the process of institutional governance because they were not concerned with making institutional beneficial decisions. Some called for rethinking the governance structures and processes, claiming that they were outdated models. Others suggested that shared governance weakened presidential leadership and made it difficult for institutions to be responsive and adaptive. All these have led to the misconception that "the current governance system virtually made inevitable the inability of institutions and systems to set priority, focus missions, and implement choices among academic programs" (Benjamin et al., 1993, as cited in Eckel, 2000), thus seriously damaging the image and abilities of faculty in their role in making good institutional decision.

2. **Barriers from Administrators:** Contemporary issues related to faculty involvement in governance have mostly arisen as a result of the distrust of administrators towards faculty in institutional decision making. Miller et al. (1996), however, found perceived lack of respect by administrators toward faculty in terms of decision-making abilities or judgment and addressed that typically faculty participation was derived from administrative options to allow faculty input into the decision-making process. In addition, Mason (1982) contended that administrators were more concerned with their own reputations and careers than to give credence to the involvement of faculty in governance. These may in part account for the insufficient faculty participation in governance on most campuses.

As institutions become larger and more complex, and are required by the changing circumstances to respond to more challenges both socially and economically, more and more administrative roles are needed and created, and the numbers and importance of managers at all levels in higher education have increased. As a result, university administrators separated themselves from the rest of the university and formed isolated councils or assemblies from faculty in which they tended to communicate only with people similar to themselves (Birnbaum, 1988). In many colleges and universities administrators do not expect to see faculty sitting in the same room where a decision is being made. Neither do they want to intrude on the territory that they believe belongs to faculty. There has been suspicion as well as a general resentment on the part of the administrators over faculty obligations to do the work of the administration (Pope & Miller, 1999). In the eyes of the administrators, Birnbaum (1988) pointed out, faculty were amateur administrators who assumed temporary administrative positions and then returned to the classroom, self-interested, unconcerned with controlling costs, or unwilling to respond to legitimate requests for accountability. In return, in the mind of the faculty, administrators were the constraints and outside pressures that seek to alter the institutions, remote from the central academic concerns that define the institutions.

3. **Barriers from Faculty Themselves:**   One of the major barriers is actually from faculty members themselves. According to Plante (1989), as early as 1940, the AAUP issued its statement of principles on academic freedom and tenure and has done a lot of work ever since to promote and defend the legitimate rights of faculty as primary decision makers in certain areas relating to academic domain. In addition, most colleges and universities have also given faculty lots of opportunities for leadership in matters on campuses, such as decisions regarding appointment, tenure, promotion of colleagues, curriculum, graduation standards, condition of employment like work load and evaluation system. However, few faculty members, especially in large universities, are involved in formulating policies regarding matters that affect student lives and the institutions, such as strategic planning, fund raising and institutional advancement, student recruitment, financial aid, and retention.

In addressing the conditions for a faculty senate's effective functioning, Weingartner (1996) pointed out that the number and quality of the persons who participated in governance activities were directly related to how effectively they could influence conditions that mattered to them and that inadequate faculty participation was a central problem in governance. According to his study, the number of faculty members who took part in senate and committee deliberations was usually too small and few participants were the campus' most successful teachers and scholars. Miller (1996) also noted that faculty involvement in a faculty forum hovered around 50% of those eligible to participate. Many faculty members did not participate because, again, they believed that administrators did not trust or give credence to faculty decision and voices. Additionally, because of the misleading belief that faculty members had better things to do than go to meetings, many faculty members preferred spending their time in studies and laboratories, rather than in conference rooms of committees.

On the other hand, some faculty participated in governance because bylaws or good politics required it. But even when they participated, faculty showed no respect for those processes, believing that governance activities were the province of mere politicians, who spoke for themselves and were therefore unable to overcome centrifugal forces (Weingartner, 1996).

Additionally, as Miller et al. (1996) pointed out, that the lack of rewards for (faculty) involvement was another serious enough problem to serve as a barrier to faculty involvement. On many campuses, chief administrators like presidents may realize the importance of faculty governance and feel it necessary to reward faculty involvement, but have not adequately provided the rewards necessary to lure the most able faculty to participate (Gilmour, 1991).

ENCOURAGE FACULTY INVOLVEMENT IN GOVERNANCE: APPROACHES AND SKILLS

In 1996, Miller et al. conducted a study to examine faculty participation in governance and identified that current trends on the college campus have not consistently reinforced the call to (faculty) involvement. Therefore, the task of immediate importance is to take more effective measures to encourage and support all faculty who wish to participate in decision making to be able to do so with ease, to give faculty more motivation for participation, and to encourage faculty to get themselves involved. In this process, while there must be improved respect and trust between administrators and faculty, campus chief administrators are a decisive factor, because, as Miller (1997) contended, strong administrative leadership has the potential to greatly reduce the participation, or conversely, to strongly increase the participation, of faculty in decision making.

To encourage faculty participation, above all, administrators must show faculty their understanding and support, and respect their input in the decision-making process. Plante (1989) pointed out that administrators who have become convinced that the development of faculty leadership is an important element of faculty development and who wish to support its promotion need only agree that leaders in academe seek creative paths to excellence and persuade others to follow these paths with enthusiasm. At the same time administrators should keep faculty informed, seek faculty's advice on all significant issues, especially those involving personnel and fiscal matters, and use their faculty's initiatives as part of the institution's strategic planning. In this way a trust of the administrators will be conveyed silently but effectively to the faculty that will stimulates faculty to take part wholeheartedly.

In consideration of seeking faculty input in campus decision making, Miller et al. (1996) and Miller (1997) pronounced that, as a primary characteristic of an ideal governance process, faculty input should be involved early in the decision-making process and faculty are to be listened to, trusted, and respected for their participation and contribution. To achieve that, administrators must be prepared to entrust major decisions to faculty representatives, be willing to see themselves as servants to the institution, and empower faculty to question decisions on policies and other issues on campus and exert their influence on the decision-making process. When faculty believe that they have the legitimate rights and responsibilities in decision making and feel that they are trusted, respected, and listened to, they will be adequately motivated and faculty involvement will be enhanced.

On the other hand, the ways administrators treat faculty affect the ways faculty react in the governance process. In the conclusion of his study of faculty roles in hard decision making, Eckel (2000) pointed out that how administrators treat faculty shapes the ways in which faculty react within the governance arena. He further addressed that when administrators act in ways consistent with trusting faculty and appreciating their special knowledge and perspectives, faculty will play active and complementary roles in governance. At the same time, however, administrators must acknowledge their roles as participants in the shared governance process.

Governance may include any activities that provide faculty opportunities to take part in decision making about the institution and its programs. In order for faculty and administrators to work cooperatively and constructively in the governance process, a positive and healthy campus climate should be created. Plante (1989) encouraged campus administrators to take it as a challenge to create a campus climate that encourages faculty to give their time and efforts generously and freely and a campus culture that should persuade as many faculty as possible that carrying a portion of the weight of shared governance is not only a noble enterprise but a civic obligation that one meets as consciously as one prepares intellectually worthwhile classes and manuscripts.

In terms of skills that can be used to enhance the roles faculty play in the decision making process, Miller (1997) identified in a national survey of faculty governance leaders nine skills that faculty leaders should master in order to exercise adequate influence on the decision-making process and to recruit more faculty in the process. These include the skill of judgment, oral communication, organizational ability, written communication, leadership, educational value, stress tolerance, problem analysis, and sensitivity. Pope and Miller (1999) found the skills were also true with faculty leaders in community colleges because they reflected a general view that group leadership has to do with identifying goals, communicating them effectively, and working to complete these tasks and objectives. In particular, they found that community college faculty leadership should focus on strong communication, organizing work, and maintaining a good balance of sensitivity between the tasks to be accomplished and the individuals involved in getting that work done. According to Pope and Miller, these tasks include creating linkages and networks for the governance unit groups and developing the data sets necessary for decision. Finally, establishing an awarding system and giving awards for participation is another effective way to lure faculty to get involved in governance.

Approaches and skills that can be used to encourage faculty to participate in governance are not effective on all campuses and should vary when used in different colleges and universities to achieve the best effect in encouraging faculty participation. Many factors, such as institutional size, may affect the ways in which faculty participate in campus decision making processes and should be taken into serious consideration. Administrators and faculty senates and councils, as well as faculty, should keep looking and try to find the best ways to involve as many faculty members as possible in the process of making good and wise institutional decisions.

CONCLUSION

Faculty involvement in shared governance is critical in the higher education administration process. However, share governance is not yet a perfect governance model and there is still much room for improvement. It needs a better understanding of the governance process, more trust between faculty and administrators, and greater efforts of both faculty and administrators. With the collaboration of the faculty and administrators and their continuous hard work, barriers to faculty participation will be removed and more faculty will be involved and take an active part in the institutional governance process and making good institutional decisions. By the time when all the faculty are fully motivated and actively involved, a more effective and successful higher education system will be presenting itself on full wings in the accomplishment of the missions and goals of all our colleges and universities.

REFERENCES

Birnbaum, R. (1988). *How college works*. San Francisco: Jossey-Bass.

Eckel, P. D. (2000). The role of shared governance in institutional hard decisions: Enable or Antagonist? *The Review of Higher Education, 24*(1), 15-39.

Gilmour, J. E. (1991). Participative governance bodies in higher education: Report of a national study. In R. Birnbaum (Ed.), *Faculty in governance: The role of senate and joint committees in academic decision making: New directions for Higher Education Report 75* (pp. 27-40). San Francisco: Jossey-Bass.

Keller, G. (1989). Shotgun marriage: The growing connection between academic management and faculty governance. In J. H. Schuster & L. H. Miller (Eds.), *Governing tomorrow's campus* (pp. 133-140). New York: Macmillan.

Mason, H. L. (1982). Four issues in contemporary campus governance. *Academe, 68*(1), 3A-14A.

Miller, M. T. (1997). Faculty governance leaders in higher education: Roles, beliefs, and skills. *Baylor Educator, 22*(1), 1-9.

Miller, M. T., McCormack, T. F., Maddox, J. F., & Seagren, A. T. (1996). Faculty participation in governance at small and large universities: Implications for practice. *Planning and Changing, 27*(3/4), 180-190.

Plante, P. R. (1989). The role of faculty in campus governance. In J. H. Schuster & L. H. Miller (Eds.), *Governing tomorrow's campus* (pp. 116-132). New York: Macmillan.

Pope, M., & Miller, M. T. (1999). The skills and tasks associated with faculty leadership in community college governance. *Journal of Applied Research in the Community College, 7*(1), 5-12.

Weingartner, R. H. (1996). *Fitting form to function: A primer on the organization of academic institutions.* Phoenix, AZ: Oryx Press.

CHAPTER 3

THE COLLEGE TRUSTEES' ROLE IN ACADEMIC GOVERNANCE

Houston Davis
Austin Peay State University

Higher education governance has undergone a dynamic shift in its locus of control in the last 40 years. Once governed locally by faculty and ceremonially by governing boards, many campuses now find themselves subject to heightened scrutiny at the state level and in many cases under direct control by state government bodies (Graham, 1989). Governing and coordinating boards are now found in all 50 states, as governments have found it necessary to establish professional bodies to direct and shape the growing systems of higher education (Graham, 1989; Hairston, 1997). The relationships between these boards, their sitting trustees, and the institutions have been further strained by the increasing involvement of elected officials in daily activities of the campuses. Elected officials have looked to the boards as a vehicle for delegated powers with intervention always an option if lawmakers deem it necessary (Hairston, 1997). This "hands-on" management arrangement has subjected board appointees to feel more allegiance to governors and legislators than to the institutions and students (Baliles, 1997). Consequently, university and community college presidents feel torn between the business perspective of board members and the established faculty culture, and the educational planning process is continually influenced by partisan politics (Baliles, 1997).

All of these issues are further compounded by shrinking state resources available to higher education due to increasing demands placed on state coffers. Increases in demand for public services have fueled much of the growth in state expenditures in the last 30 years. Bonser, McGregor, and Oster (1996) stated that some of the reasons for the increase in demands on state revenues are demographic changes, growing populations, income growth, income redistribution, and risk aversion. Echoing the thoughts of Graham (1989), Marcus found that demands placed on the systems by the G.I. Bill and the baby-boom enrollment were the driving forces of change (1997). Mills (1999) and Eckel (2000) point to rapid pace of change faced by higher education in such areas as information technology, restricted funding, expansions in the economy, and multiple stakeholders as the driving forces behind challenges facing higher education and other public sectors.

Charges of a lack of accountability have stepped up the demands on higher education leaders and fueled calls for postsecondary reform across the country (Davis, 2002). An Association of Governing Boards (AGB) study revealed that most political leaders want strong and effective governing boards, but feel that intervention is currently needed (Association of Governing Boards [AGB], 1999). Most governing board members take their responsibilities seriously, but too many political obstacles stand in their way. Among legislative leaders there is strong support for governance by lay board members, but concerns abound for the current performance of these groups (1999). Problems noted by the AGB study were placed into three categories: serving the public interest, negotiation of the political environment, and increasing board responsiveness (1999). In the foreseeable future, more state level involvement rather than less should be expected by those charged with leading postsecondary institutions. Bowen et al. (1997) found that state boards that are both part of higher education and part of state government are more successful at balancing public interests and institutional concerns than solely institutional governing boards. However, regardless of the formal governance arrangement, higher education officials (especially trustees and presidents) must understand the dynamics of power and tension that comes from the competition between local autonomy and statewide governance controls.

Daugbjerg and Marsh (1998) posit that "policy outcomes are not just a function of what occurs in the network; they are also strongly influenced by the economic, political, and ideological context within which the network operates" (p. 54). The tension's resulting from the state's demands for accountability and higher education's consistent desire for freedom and autonomy are perhaps best examined in Berdahl's work (1990). From

Berdahl's perspective, both sides are expecting too much and really do not understand the true concerns of each side (1990). Defining autonomy as "the power to govern without outside controls" and accountability as "the requirement to demonstrate responsible actions" (1990, p. 38), Berdahl posits that each side should realize that a balance is ideal. Sabloff (1997) characterizes the struggle between autonomy and accountability to be a fact of life that has always existed and will probably always be a force in higher education concerns. State legislatures are much more specialized and informed now than they have been in the past (Greer, 1986; Sabloff, 1997; Weaver & Geske, 1997). Legislative members have increased their staff numbers and devoted themselves to much more of a year-round schedule of activities (Sabloff, 1997). The establishment of legislative standing committees has combined with governing and coordinating boards to create a constant regulatory environment for the individual campuses (Davis, 2002). Because of the myriad of benefits to be gained through a quality higher education system, the stakes have also been raised regarding cooperation between business interests, state government, and the campus expertise. The public and private benefits earlier outlined support the argument that a greater emphasis must be placed on an educated citizenry (Jones, Ewell, & McGuinness, 1998). As the global economy has put a premium on knowledge capital rather than manufacturing skills, employers and government officials are demanding more of higher education than ever (Jones et al., 1998).

POLITICS OF HIGHER EDUCATION GOVERNANCE

Education has been a point of contention in America since the initiation of publicly funded schools in the Massachusetts colony in 1647 (Dye, 1969). Individualists were against the idea of taxing citizens for the education of another person's child and elitists were opposed to the notion of arming commoners with knowledge (1969). Elementary, secondary, and higher education are firmly involved in politics and always will be (Gove, 1971). Adding to the pressure is education's position as second only to national defense as the country's largest fiscal responsibility and its role as the most costly function of state governments (Dye, 1969). As far back as the early 1970s, higher education was predicted to fall in line with other divisions of state government in having to fight for their piece of dwindling state resources (Gove, 1971). Gove accurately forecast that higher education would not continue to be seen as the fourth branch of state government. In fact, research during the mid-1970s found an increase in governmental output associated with higher education (Jacob, 1976).

Among sectors of state government activity, higher education was the only one displaying increased activity rather than stable or declining (1976).

The postwar baby boom and explosion of higher education the 1960s led to much more desire of state leaders to acquire more control of higher education matters (Graham, 1989). During that time of growth, states created many of the coordinating and governing boards that exist today (North Carolina Center for Public Policy Research [NCCPPR], 2000; Davis, 2002). Though created in attempts to bring order and accountability to higher education, states have in some cases just extended the political umbrella by "allowing higher education (governance and coordinating boards) to become the centerpiece of top-level patronage politics and public score settling" (Graham, 1989, p. 93). Modeled primarily after the boards of trustees that have traditionally led private institutions, governing and coordinating boards have become permanent fixtures on the higher education map (McGuinness, 1997). Approximately 65% of students attend postsecondary schools that are a part of a multicampus system (1997). As of 2000, state higher education governance structures basically fell into three categories: consolidated governing board systems, coordinating board systems, and planning agency systems (NCCPPR, 2000). Under consolidated governing board systems, governance is centralized in one or two governing bodies. Currently 24 states operate under this model (2000). Coordinating board systems are also found in 24 states and provide for a liaison body between state government and the governing boards of individual institutions (2000). Planning agency structures are only found in two states (Delaware and Michigan). These agencies coordinate communication and planning with little direct authority over the institutions or their governing boards.

As stated earlier, governing and coordinating boards grew out of state government's desire for a rational system of postsecondary education delivery (Moos & Rourke, 1959; Graham, 1989; Marcus, 1997). Set up to deal with the interests of the day, those interests have shifted over time and the struggle between centralization and decentralization has grown (Marcus, 1997). McGuinness (1997) charged that the most perplexing issue facing lawmakers is how to position the higher education system to take on the changes brought by a more market-driven economy. Wrestling with concerns for issues such as mission clarity, technology infrastructure, and increasing political control is becoming commonplace in state-level higher education planning across the country. These worries of governors and legislators are not just much ado about nothing and are not concerns that have crept up overnight. In their seminal piece on the campus and state policy environment, Moos & Rourke (1959) stated that properly positioning the public higher education system within the overall system of government has always been a problem. Benjamin and Carroll (1996) conducted survey research that found a common problem within governance structures of not being able to tie resource allocation to mission. Instead of being able to focus scarce resources to areas of weakness or strengths, funding is spread uniformly to all disciplines, programs, and institutions within a system (1996). Calls for accountability are based on the problems of current bureaucracies, ambiguous priorities, and fragmented powers inherent to the status quo in higher education governance in many states (1996). McGuinness (1997) encourages state leaders to continue to examine their governance and coordinating structures to determine whether changes are overdue. In the last 20 years, just about every state has reevaluated its higher education system in terms of quality, accountability, and efficiency (Marcus, 1997). There seems to be conflicting desires as elected officials have expected governing boards to meet public interests and set direction for higher education while the institutions have wanted the governing boards to be advocates for funding and keep the politics at a minimum (McGuinness, Epper, & Arredondo, 1994; Marcus, 1997).

CURRENT STATE OF HIGHER EDUCATION GOVERNANCE

M. W. Peterson (1985) states that studying higher education as an organization is challenging because of the changing locus of control that has occurred. Higher education institutions have for most of their histories been governed by a sense of internal control with authority largely falling to the faculty and administration of the single institution (1985). These institutions represent professional bureaucracies in which faculty seek control of their work and also seek to have a voice in the decisions affecting their lives (Mintzberg, 1979). In comparison to the more common machine bureaucracy form of business and industry, these professional networks are based on mutual respect and dedication to the community (1979). This rare form of organizational structure and control causes particular stress to elected officials accustomed to looking to profits for measures of success (Sabloff, 1997). Dill (1982) attempts to show that the growing movement toward applying business models of organization to higher education has not held onto the affects of culture on the organization. Dill (1982) charges that these rational processes can abandon beliefs and meaning that tie an organization's history to its coordinated future. Especially during times of declining resources, it is argued that higher education leaders should attempt to nurture faculty and community to avoid conflict and loss of morale. Dill (1982) is also quick to note that the short-term strategies of efficiency experts will not yield long-term productivity, commitment, and loyalty of the membership of the academic community.

According to M. W. Peterson (1985), some time around the mid-1970s institutions became much more aware of the growing external forces that were less controlled and much less understood by the campus community. It was at this time that governing boards and publicly elected officials began exercising greater authority in the name of accountability. In the 1980s governors and legislators began seeking even more control over institutions through quality initiatives (McGuinness, 1997). Governors and legislators began expecting these higher education boards to exercise firm control of the institutions rather than working as advocates for them (Millett, 1984, as cited in Graham, 1989). As a result of giving new responsibilities and authority to the governing and coordinating boards, more opportunities for friction with the campus were created (McGuinness, 1997). Mortimer & McConnell (1978) characterized these trends toward efficiency and accountability as being phenomenon that would last through the 1980s and beyond. Until this shift, faculty had a much more successful role in academic governance because local leadership largely shaped the control and mission of campuses (1978). In order for shared governance to exist on a campus, it must be based on some level of commitment to coordination between faculty desires, campus interests, and state-level concerns.

This competition between the interests of the universities and the policy demands of the state form the basis for current studies of postsecondary governance. As mentioned earlier, the stakes are high because of the level to which higher education contributes to the economy of the state (Association for Governing Boards [AGB], 1999). Legislative concerns are real and have a dynamic impact on the flow of ideas within the higher education policy domain. Greer (1986) examined the political environment surrounding higher education planning and found that legislative norms concerning the importance of higher education, levels of independence from regulations, and authorities of individual legislators are all significant in policy formation and outcomes.

Sabloff (1997) argues that the relationship between state government and the institutions has always had aspects of the autonomy versus accountability debate. Throughout the last half of the twentieth century, regulations have increased that have inevitably stripped away institutional rights to govern themselves (1997). Institutions have had to accept some level of state-control as a necessary evil. Sabloff (1997) speaks to the political transformation that state governments have gone through in the last twenty years. She points to year round activities, increased staff, career politicians, increasing education levels of officials, and standing committees as evidence of a changing system of governance over all state programs and services (1997). State government is experiencing what has been called at the federal level a "professionalization" of the legislative body (Polsby, 1975; Squire, 1992). Concern is evident that political leaders and their political appointees are increasingly moving into the day-to-day activities of higher education. The establishment of legislative standing committees has combined with governing and coordinating boards to create a constant regulatory environment for the individual campuses. Though higher education may not get caught up in partisan politics as much as other areas of government, it is constantly part of a political process (Baliles, 1997).

With massive turnover in federal and state government elections in 1994, the instability of leadership in state government had a great impact on the turnover of commission members and trustees in the late 1990s (McGuinness, 1997). Turnover of leadership hurts boards because of the institutional knowledge lost and the increased chance of politics making its way into board decisions (1997). Though political leaders try to step in and provide stability and direction, their entry more often than not allows "political rather than educational values [to] dominate the debate" (1997, p. 3). Higher education officials and scholars have been forced to adjust to the increasing activities and involvement. As noted in a recent study of higher education governance restructuring, when relationships between government and higher education systems become more strained, the likelihood of government becoming more involved increases (Marcus, 1997).

EMERGENCE OF A NEW GOVERNANCE LAYER

Since 1990 an estimated 21 states have established state-level governmental advisory groups with similar charges of bettering higher education in their respective states (Mills, 1999). Whether as a sensible policy development tool or as the latest fad in government (Bennett, 1991; Kerr, 1983, as cited in Howlett & Ramesh, 1995), these commissions—drawn primarily from elected leaders, top higher education officials, and politically-connected citizens—shaped much of the public policy debate surrounding higher education in the last decade. These groups played a significant role in states where the existing governing and coordinating boards were criticized for inactivity or lack of leadership (Mills, 1999; Davis, 2002). In many cases these adhoc coordinating boards infringed on some of the responsibilities and duties of existing trustee bodies thereby creating another layer of governance, if only temporary (Davis, 2002).

Executive advisory boards or study commissions are vehicles that have been used for years by federal and state government officials in debating matters surrounding areas such as education, health care, and environmental policy (Davis, 2002). Though created under the guise of action, reform, or change, these groups have earned poor reputations as evasive bodies looking to provide cover for executives and avoid taking substantive actions (Wolanin, 1975). To the contrary, Wolanin's research found that these groups exist to "formulate domestic policies and to facilitate their adoption" (1975, p. 11). Nevertheless, executive advisory councils live with the stigma of being weak public policy vehicles that serve as political cover for elected officials looking to move on to other issues (1975).

In his descriptive study of the activities of 21 states' higher education advisory councils, Mills (1999) defines these higher education policy entities as "specially constituted groups with a majority of its members from outside the higher education system and a broad charge allowing them to take a comprehensive look at the structure and operation of all public higher education in the state" (p. 3). Though these entities are not the only planning mechanisms in higher education, they do "claim an atmosphere where independent citizens can work along with higher education and government representatives to deal with problems and policy issues" (Mills, 1999, p. 3).

Bringing together these diverse interests however is not seen by all to be a positive step toward productive discussion. In a claim that could also be made against formal trustee and regent bodies, Doyle and Trombley (1998) charge that all the competing interests and already busy business leaders can result in watered-down debate and study. Critics also lash out at the tendency of these groups to have their membership stacked by a governor with people that are just there to advance a particular agenda (Mills, 1999). Doyle and Trombley (1998) though assert that this arrangement might be the most productive course, as governors can find members who know what he/she wants done and can set out on a course to see that those changes are formally endorsed by the advisory commission.

In exploring why these ad hoc groups' recommendations are not likely to be sustained, Doyle and Trombley refer to the tradition of government bodies using blue-ribbon study groups to deal with short-term political problems (1998). Critics have certainly emerged of the effectiveness of these councils in spurring or promoting change. Doyle and Trombley (1998) point out that it is rare for these bodies to make a great impact on higher education. In fairness to executive advisory commissions, Wolanin (1975) points out that their recommendations are by their nature advisory. No changes in policy or governmental structure can occur without other factors and influences coming into play (Wolanin, 1975). Because the "completion of the report and the termination of the commission are synonymous ... the reports and recommendations are orphans" (1975, p. 157). Though Mills' (1999) work focuses on what the councils reported rather than the *how and why* of policy adoption and implementation, he still poses questions about how effective these groups are at shaping and directing policy. Johnson and Marcus (1986, as cited in Mills, 1999) conducted a study concerned with how commissions contribute to change and reached conclusions that these groups could be positive problem-solvers. Critics, however, point to the lack of rigor of the policy analysis done by the groups and charge that the reports tend to avoid recommending fundamental changes and neglect implementation strategy (P. E. Peterson, 1985, as cited in Mills, 1999). Mills (1999) defends the commissions against these allegations by pointing out that the groups are generally called to deal with ambiguous issues that do not lend themselves to straightforward planning. These groups faced broad charges and thus came forward with concerns and recommendations that though large in scope were no less important to the future of the states.

UNDERSTANDING THE EXTERNAL FACTORS ASSOCIATED WITH HIGHER EDUCATION POLICY

Some scholars maintain that actions taken by policy makers depend on the political, economic, and social environments in which they operate (Howlett & Ramesh, 1995). Most agree that few organizational decisions are made in a vacuum and those decisions will inevitably influence or be influenced by outside entities (Horowitz, 1990). These external factors influence the ability of the state (or the campus) to develop good policy (Howlett & Ramesh, 1995). To an extent, the environment can restrict the freedom of a policy-making body and may cripple the body's unity and coherence. Therefore, the importance of understanding the full compliment of factors influencing higher education policy is as important as weighing the pros and cons of the actual policy. Unlike other public policy domains, higher education studies boast very little literature on the political and economic processes that form and shape the enterprise.

In their research on the politics of policy formation, Desaie, Holden, and Shelley (1998) charge that strong policy research must place "the processes and outcomes of policymaking within appropriate political contexts" (p. 432). The events and decisions of yesterday drive higher education policy and governance decisions as much as they are spurred by conditions of today. Attempts at studying the policy processes of higher education reform must tie political events to the origins of the circumstances and decisions influencing change. Higher education reforms seem to avoid the court of public opinion in that they are rarely hot-button, political issues, but they are still subject to several external tests of their strength and worth (Davis, 2002). Higher education advocates at the local (campus) level must recognize external and internal forces and

respect the impact that these forces have on the matriculation of proposals into the arena of high politics. Internal factors such as having a policy
champion and high-quality policy entrepreneurs are crucial to higher
education proposals gaining momentum toward adoption. Without the
key people lined up to carry the load and protect the ideas from outside
threats, reform initiatives will rarely move beyond becoming shelf material.

Trustees and governance leaders are, for better or worse, the link that
universities and colleges have to the decision-making arena in which high
politics are played. Higher education regents and trustees are assigned to
their posts through political vehicles and wield a great deal of authority.
Decisions made by these board members profoundly affect many individuals and businesses (Holmes, 1996). Faculty members' academic careers,
students' educational opportunities, academic programming, and economic development initiatives are all subjects of discussion and decision
at board meetings (1996). Because trustees take on this legislative function, they are routinely caught in a web of conflicts and interests (Hayes,
1982). Expected to represent multiple views and reach compromise, the
trustee is consistently in the unenviable position of working toward solutions that serve the overall interests of the state's system of higher education (1982).

REFERENCES

Association of Governing Boards. (1999). *Bridging the gap between state government
and higher education.* Washington, DC: Author.
Baliles, G. L. (1997, Fall). Partisan political battles: Governing boards and university presidents are plagued by divided loyalties. *National Crosstalk* [On-line],
5(17). Available; http://www.highereducation.org/crosstalk/index.shtml
Benjamin, R., & Carroll, S. J. (1996). Impediments and imperatives in restructuring higher education. *Education Administration Quarterly, 32,* 705-720.
Bennett, C. J. (1991). What is policy convergence and what causes it? *British Journal of Political Science, 21*(2), 215.
Berdahl, R. (1990). Public universities and state governments: Is the tension
benign? *Educational Record, 71*(1), 38-42.
Bonser, C. F., McGregor, Jr., E. B., & Oster, Jr., C. V. (1996). *Policy choices and public
action.* Englewood Cliffs, NJ: Prentice-Hall.
Bowen, F. M., Bracco, K. R., Callan, P. M., Finney, J. E., Richardson, R. C., &
Trombley, W. (1997). *State structures for the governance of higher education: A com-
parative study.* Research paper for the California Higher Education Policy
Center. Sacramento: California Higher Education Policy Center.
Daugbjerg, C., & Marsh, D. (1998). Explaining policy outcomes: Integrating the
policy network approach with macro-level and micro-level analysis. In

D. Marsh (Ed.), *Comparing policy networks* (pp. 52-74). Buckingham, United Kindom: Open University Press.

Davis, H. (2002). *A political model of higher education governance and policy reform adoption* (IHELG Monograph Series, 02-06). Houston, TX: The Insititute for Higher Education Law & Governance.

Desaie, U., Holden, M., & Shelley, M. (1998). The politics of policy: Prospects and realities. *Policy Studies Journal, 26*(3), 423-433.

Dill, D. D. (1982). The management of academic culture: Notes on the management of meaning and social integration. *Higher Education, 11*, 303-320.

Doyle, W., & Trombley, W. (1998, Spring). Tennessee's bid for national prominence: "Blue-ribbon" study group faces a formidable task." *National CrossTalk* [On-line], *6*(2). Available: http://www.highereducation.org/crosstalk/index.shtml

Dye, T. R. (1969). *Politics in states and communities.* Englewood Cliffs, NJ: Prentice-Hall.

Eckel, P. D. (2000). The role of shared governance in institutional hard decisions: Enabler or antagonist? *The Review of Higher Education, 24*(1), 15-39.

Gove, S. K. (1971). The politics of higher education. In J. A. Reidel (Ed.), *New perspectives in state and local politics* (pp. 285-295). Waltham, MA: Xerox College.

Graham, H. D. (1989). Structure and governance in American higher education: Historical and comparative analysis in state policy. *Journal of Policy History, 1*(1), 80-106.

Greer, D. G. (1986). Politics and higher education: The strategy of state-level coordination and policy implementation. In S. K. Gove & T. M. Stauffer (Eds.), *Policy controversies in higher education* (pp. 27-50). New York: Greenwood.

Hairston, E. H. (1997, Fall). Political passages: The relationship of politics and higher education. *National Crosstalk* [On-line], *5*(3). Available: http://www.highereducation.org/crosstalk/index.shtml

Hayes, R. (Ed.). (1982, June). *Ethics and government.* Proceedings of Annual Chief Justice Earl Warren Conference, Washington, DC.

Holmes, A. B. (1996). *Ethics in higher education: Case studies for regents.* Norman, OK: University of Oklahoma Press.

Horowitz, I. (Ed.). (1990). Introduction. In *Organization and decision theory* (pp. 1-12). Boston: Kluwer Academic.

Howlett, M., & Ramesh, M. (1995). *Studying public policy: Policy cycles and policy subsystems.* Toronto, Canada: Oxford University Press.

Jacob, H. (1976). Public policy in the American states. In H. Jacob & K. N. Vines (Eds.), *Politics in the American states: A comparative analysis* (3rd ed.). Boston: Little Brown.

Johnson, J., & Marcus, L. (1986). *Blue ribbon commissions and higher education: Changing academe from the outside* (ASHE-ERIC Higher Education Report #2). Washington, DC: Association for the Study of Higher Education.

Jones, D., Ewell, P., & McGuinness, A. (1998). *The challenges and opportunities facing higher education: An agenda for policy research.* San Jose, CA: National Center for Public Policy and Higher Education.

Kerr, C. (1983). *The future of industrial societies: convergence or continuing diversity?* Cambridge, MA: Harvard University Press.

Marcus, L. R. (1997). Restructuring state higher education governance patterns. *The Review of Higher Education, 20*(4), 399-418.

McGuinness, A. C., Epper, R. M., & Arredondo, S. (1994). *State postsecondary structures handbook.* Denver, CO: Education Commission of the States.

McGuinness, A. C., Jr. (1997, Fall). A complex relationship: State coordination and governance of higher education. *National CrossTalk* [On-line], *5*(3). Available: http://www.highereducation.org/crosstalk/index.shtml.

Millett, J. D. (1984). *Conflict in higher education: State governance coordination versus institutional independence.* San Francisco: Jossey-Bass.

Mills, M. (1999, November). *Stories of excellence and enterprise in higher education policy making: A narrative analysis of the reports of blue ribbon commissions on higher education.* Paper presented at the Annual Meeting of Association for the Study of Higher Education, San Antonio, TX.

Mintberg, H. (1991). The professional bureaucracy. In M. W. Peterson (Ed.), *Organization and governance in higher education* (4th ed., pp. 53-75). Needham Heights, MA: Simon & Schuster.

Moos, M., & Rourke, F. E. (1959). *The campus and the state.* Baltimore: The Johns Hopkins Press.

Mortimor, K. P., & McConnell, T. R. (Eds.). (1978). Process of academic governance. In *Sharing authority effectively* (pp. 266-284). San Francisco: Jossey-Bass.

North Carolina Center for Public Policy Research. (2000). *Governance and coordination of public higher education in all fifty states.* Raleigh, NC: Author.

Peterson, M. W. (1985). Postsecondary organization theory and research: Fragmentation or integration. *Educational Researcher, 14*, 3.

Peterson, P. E. (1985). Did the education commissions say anything?" *Education and Urban Society, 17*(2), 126-144.

Polsby, N. W. (1975). Legislatures. In F. I. Greenstein & N. W. Polsby (Eds.), *Handbook of poltical science: Government institutions and processes* (Vol. 5, pp. 257-320). Reading, MA: Addison-Wesley.

Sabloff, P. L. (1997). Another reason why state legislatures will continue to restrict public university autonomy. *The Review of Higher Education, 20*, 2.

Squire, P. (1992). Legislative professionals and membership diversity in state legislatures. *Legislative Studies Quarterly, 17*(1), 69-79.

Weaver, S. W., & Geske, T. G. (1997). Educational policy making in the state legislature: Legislator as policy expert. *Educational Policy, 11*(3), 309-329.

Wolanin, T. (1975). *Presidential advisory commissions: Truman to Nixon.* Madison, WI: The University of Wisconsin Press.

PART II

GOVERNANCE WITHIN THE ACADEMIC ORGANIZATION

CHAPTER 4

LEADERSHIP IN FACULTY GOVERNANCE

Choice, Mandate, and Default

Michael T. Miller
University of Arkansas

Myron L. Pope
University of Alabama

The concept of faculty participation in governance is grounded partially in the administrative desire to build consensus throughout the organization and partially in the thinking that faculty have a right to involvement in governance. The question of right becomes increasingly complex as institutions make references to the American Association of University Professors (AAUP) guidelines which display a right of faculty to involvement in such areas as admissions and curricular content, although legal cases alternatively restrict, in strict definition, the involvement of faculty in shared governance. The environment has led to numerous disputes about the rights and privileges of faculty and administrators in shared decision making.

The concept of governance has become a central theme in the examination, study, and practice of higher education. Something other than

Policy and University Faculty Governance, 45–57
Copyright © 2003 by Information Age Publishing

"management" and "academic leadership," governance relates to the process and product of creating policy and making decisions related to the welfare of the college campus. Governance is also central to the larger theme of state or system-level coordination of the higher education enterprise, a coordination often predicated on individual agendas, political positioning, and pork-barrel politics. On campus, for governance to be shared, there must be a recognition of trust and importance, reasoning and logic, and willingness to confide in the ability of others.

This backdrop creates an environment that has traditionally relegated shared governance to specific policy areas. This traditional approach has been and continues to be the source of difficulty for many faculty cogovernance units and groups. This tradition, the binding culture of placing the governing body within a specific framework of authority, both creates and reinforces the power of shared authority. Quite literally, faculty involvement in governance is dictated by institutional culture. Miller and Seagren (1993), in what later turned out to be the initial National Data Base on Faculty Involvement in Governance (NDBFIG) research project, identified the issue of trust between faculty and administrators as perhaps the most resistant barrier to shared authority.

Replete with challenges to personal and professional livelihood, time constraints, disappointment, and elation, each year hundreds of faculty are elected and appointed by their peers to serve in various leadership roles among faculty groups. These individuals, typically termed chairs, presidents, lead faculty members, governor, and so on, lead a host of faculty governance bodies, such as "senates," "forums," or "councils." Using Gilmour's (1991) estimation that 90% of all colleges and universities utilize some form of faculty governance unit, more than 2,000 faculty members assume their version of the faculty senate presidency each year.

The exact number of shared governance units may never be fully comprehended. There is, however, a general acceptance that faculty members do voluntarily see a benefit to shared governance, and feel strongly enough about the process and results that they sacrifice their time, energy, and devotion to these faculty governance units. As an exploration into why, how, and who participates in these governance bodies as leaders, the current chapter was developed to explore in greater detail the concept of faculty governance unit leadership. Specifically, efforts were made to identify meaningful data that can be helpful in both the internal management of shared governance bodies and in assisting governance units in better understanding their operation, effectiveness, and success. The data drawn for the chapter has been taken from the National Data Base on Faculty Involvement in Governance Project, which is described in greater detail later.

DEFINING FACULTY COGOVERNANCE

Faculty involvement in governance is a fundamental concept no longer unique to higher education. The private sector of business and industry has embraced quality management precepts that dictate the involvement of specialists and highly educated workers in the creation and implementation of policy and general decision making, a trend colleges and universities have actively followed. Faculty involvement in governance activities has been identified in the earliest colleges and universities in the United States, and repeatedly, the activity has been described as processural, dependent on the process of involvement to create feelings of ownership and acceptance in decision making (Floyd, 1985).

Faculty involvement typically takes the form of a governance unit, such as an intended representative democracy called a senate, an open town-hall like forum, or similar body of faculty who gather to discuss, debate, and resolve questions of policy and make decisions. The extent to which these bodies can be held accountable to the decision-making process is somewhat questionable, as some legal interpretation argues that there is no legal basis for faculty involvement in governance, and that specifically administrators have no right to request faculty to make decisions or act beyond the bounds of teaching courses (Miles, 1997). Citing *Minnesota v. Knight* (1984) and *Connick v. Myers* (1983), Miles argued that faculty do not have a legal right to criticize their employer on administrative decision making, and that this subsequently encumbers the faculty member's ability to be involved in making strategic decisions for the college.

The ability of a faculty senate or similar governance unit to effectively function has been noted by both scholars and practitioners alike, yet the value of the organizations to serve as forums for debate has been noted (Baldridge, 1982; Birnbaum, 1991). Miller (1997) described the functioning of one such faculty forum, and noted low participation rates and few substantive action items. The NDBFIG initiative revealed few differences between the roles of faculty in cogovernance between research-oriented and teaching-oriented faculty (Miller, McCormack, Maddox, & Seagren, 1996), noted that teachers believe they do a better job when they are involved in governance (Miller, Garavalia, & McCormack, 1996), and that the process of sharing authority has a great deal to do with how decisions can be accepted (Miller & Kang, 1999).

The key to these governance units, however, is the lead, elected, or appointed faculty member who has the ability to provide group direction. These faculty leaders provide the pace, tenor, and tone of the particular faculty senate or governance unit, and subsequently define the group as being active or reactive, progressive or isolationist, willing to take risks or willing to hold the course. These leaders also have the potential to demonstrate and profess the extent to which group decisions are accepted and to what extent the senate provides a meaningful recommendation or challenge to the decision-making process and outcome.

COGOVERNANCE BARRIERS AND BENEFITS

Governance activities are laced with positive and negative experiences, expectations, and results. Often, shared governance allows for greater employee ownership and commitment to decisions, serving as a direct result of sharing in the process of finding creative solutions to often difficult problems. Joint ownership in governance activities can build trust between faculty and administrators, can break down communication barriers based on personalities or job classifications, and can aid in the development of a collegial atmosphere. Conversely, shared governance can greatly slow the decision-making process, and the simple adding of individuals to the decision-making process does not guarantee a broader array of solutions. Shared governance, based generally on the principle of team-work, can and often does result in feelings of competition, argumentation, and resentment. Although faculty may enjoy being heard in the search for solutions, failure to accept their solutions or directions can do substantial damage to the work environment.

Effective shared governance relies on a structure that allows input at various points in the decision-making process, but as Miller and Seagren (1993) noted, it is often the culture of decision making that serves as a barrier to effective collaboration. Evans (1999) noted that one of the greatest barriers to faculty involvement in higher education governance has to do with feelings of powerlessness among faculty. If the concerns, voices, and ideas of faculty are not processed, then faculty are less likely to make an effort to be involved and the environment feeds on itself to the point of exclusiveness in decision making. Effective shared governance bodies are those that allow faculty to participate in decision making, making reasoned, well-informed and well-educated recommendations that are at the very least considered and processed by both other faculty and senior-level administrators. Faculty body recommendations need not always be implemented, but the serious consideration of serious faculty recommendations can be vital to effective broad-based decision making. The added logical extension of effective faculty governance, then, is the reliance on unit leaders who can usher the strength of the body toward "effectiveness."

TYPES OF SENATE LEADERS

There are generally several types of individuals who assume the primary leadership role in a senate or similar governance unit. Trow (1990) argued that leadership in faculty governance units is largely reactive and based on a collective spirit of challenging administrators. This notion of adversarial relationships between faculty governance and administration is relatively traditional and does not suggest a broad-based, contemporary view of representativeness. Indeed, some faculty governance leaders may well assume positions of leadership and responsibility in an effort to build experiences to assume positions of greater responsibility beyond faculty identity (Westerfield, 1997). Governance unit leaders tend to have unique experience bases and perspectives and suggested here are a representative listing of rationales and depictions of leaders based on political role theory. Faculty governance unit leaders can be perceived as:

Rear Guard: These faculty senate leaders see themselves as the appendage to the larger faculty, charged with protecting the body with their own sacrifice. Often serving as a watchdog to campus administration, they operate as a loosely defined or organized collection of faculty who would willingly give up their comfort for the welfare of the campus and the faculty at large.

- *Politician*:   Also seen as a "politico," these leaders see themselves as the future leaders of the campus and administration. Deriving their perceived power from the ability to organize and amass the influence of the collective faculty, these leaders find fulfillment in the process of negotiating between administrators and the faculty governance unit. These leaders are primarily concerned with power relationships.
- *Puppet*:   These governance leaders find their own hope, aspirations, and enjoyment of the process of shared governance from gaining the approval of campus administration. Drawing largely on the college administration for agenda items, these individuals are reactionary in nature and often see diplomacy as their trademark characteristic in brokering decisions between the faculty and administration.
- *Rebel*:   Also seen as the "vigilante," these concerned faculty find some enjoyment in the open challenging of administrations, trustees, and even faculty groups which appear compliant to administrative interests. These faculty leaders typically see themselves as the true defenders of faculty interests, and concentrate their efforts on taking preemptive actions and challenging administrative actions.

- *Tactician*:   Also seen as the faculty governance unit "mechanic," these leaders play out their roles as those most concerned about the process rather than the content of decisions. Primarily focusing agenda setting and establishing the tenor, tone, and pace of activity, these individuals often see their role as one of surviving the elected term.
- *Idealist*:   These individuals draw tremendous personal fulfillment from the action of being involved and the actual participation in governance activities. These leaders are more likely to be discriminating in selecting issues to challenge and support, have excellent participation records, and feel an obligation to the institution is being served. They see service as "their turn," and comply.

Although most faculty governance unit leaders will be amalgamations of these types, most have a similar characteristic: they do not see themselves as representative of one group to a large group. In only rare occasions do faculty senators or similar leaders rely on town hall meetings or electronic forums to find out how to vote on key issues. Faculty governance is generally expected, but not fully respected. The result is the creation of a system, which supports a particular culture and faculty leadership style; a style reinforced through participation and elections that support particular ways of thinking and acting.

THE NATIONAL DATA BASE PROJECT

The National Data Base on Faculty Involvement in Governance (NDB-FIG) Project was developed in 1994 at The University of Alabama's (UA) College of Education. The project, which originally began as a collaborative research effort between the higher education programs at the University of Nebraska–Lincoln and UA initially focused on differentials between tenured and nontenured faculty in choosing to participate in shared governance activities. With the aid of several grants, a survey instrument was developed dealing with the current role of governance and identifying an ideal governance process. The survey was ultimately distributed on 55 different college campuses (including major research universities, doctoral universities, comprehensive universities, private liberal arts colleges, comprehensive community colleges, and technical colleges) and resulted in over 4,000 responses. These institutions became known as NDBFIG participants, with a variety of consulting reports and in-service programs developed for each. Many of the findings of various phases of the project have been cited in this chapter.

Over the five year existence of the NDBFIG, leaders at these 55 institutions were asked to nominate other faculty governance unit leaders for participation in a study of their characteristics. With over 200 respondents to this phase of the project, some of the findings are presented here as an exploratory portrait of who is participating in governance bodies, what they get out of the process, and why they choose to be involved in such high-profile positions.

WHO LEADS FACULTY GOVERNANCE UNITS?

As Gilmour (1991) noted, most faculty governance unit leaders are elected by their peers, although there are many variations on the model. Some institutions allow for presidential selection of governance body leaders, while others utilize competitive, party-like elections with formal nomination procedures. Institutional culture, as advocated and defined by Birnbaum (1988), certainly play a role in this type of environment. One such recent example of institutional culture was the case of the approval and acceptance of a bargaining unit at Southern Illinois University at Carbondale, where leadership facilitated the larger faculty interests after a period of time where there had been an initial rejection of unionization (Magney, 1999).

The NDBFIG project was primarily interested in five dimensions to the faculty governance unit leader: motivation to serve or be elected, role orientation in serving in the position, skills required to succeed in the position, tasks undertaken as a leader, and general career futures, intended to provide some extension of the motivation. Based on survey responses, each of these areas are subsequently highlighted.

Motivation to Serve

Motivation in general and specific terms is difficult to isolate and measure as a variable. People, particularly professionals who commit their livelihood to one of academic service, often view participation as a form of responsibility. Many faculty senate leaders see their personal stories as a demonstration of their motivation, stories such as protection of academic integrity, support or challenge to administrators at various levels, and out of professional obligation.

The strongest motivation for involvement was found to be empowerment (see Table 1). The concept of empowerment relates to the ability for faculty, both as individuals and collectively, to control the fate and future of the institution. In a sense, empowerment identifies the faculty leader

Table 1.   Faculty Governance Leader Motivations (N =185)

Motivator	Mean Rating	(SD)	Rank
Empowerment	4.23	(.87)	1
Sense of responsibility	4.16	(.69)	2
Importance of decision making	4.07	(1.01)	3
Asked to participate	4.00	(1.27)	4
Sense of professionalism	3.99	(.84)	5
Sense of ownership	3.92	(1.00)	6
Campus environment	3.90	(1.10)	7

with the future, goals, and objectives of the institution. Strong motivations for faculty involvement also included a sense of responsibility, importance of decision making, being asked to participate, sense of professionalism, sense of ownership, and in response to a campus environment that encouraged, or discouraged, participation.

Orientations

Just over half (51%) of all faculty governance leaders involved in NDB-FIG activities identified themselves as being "process oriented" rather than "task oriented" (45%) while serving as an elected leader. The concept of process orientation relates to the idea that elected leaders are interested and guided by the notion of following procedure and ushering legislation or motions properly through the guidelines of a senate.

This notion is not in opposition but does not support the concept of an issue orientation. Somewhat intertwined with the "task" orientation identification, faculty leaders who engage and embrace a career of service to and with certain issues are in the minority. In a sense, true both with local and national politics, single-issue candidates and politicians have relatively shorter political careers.

Skills for Leadership

Faculty governance leaders rely on a number of skills that are applicable to both administrators and faculty serving in quasi-administrative positions. As shown in Table 2, the NDBFIG research project identified that the most needed skill for a faculty senate president was sound judgement. Sound judgement is a multidimensional skill, requiring the leadership

Table 2.   Skills for Faculty Governance Unit Leadership (N = 180)

Skill	Mean Rating	(SD)	Rank
Judgement	4.50	(.74)	1
Oral communication skills	4.21	(.63)	2
Organizational ability	4.21	(.89)	3
Written communication skills	4.02	(1.00)	4
Leadership	4.00	(1.01)	5
Educational values	4.00	(.99)	6
Stress tolerance	3.99	(1.00)	7
Problem analysis	3.92	(1.01)	8
Sensitivity	3.89	(1.28)	9

individual to ascribe to a certain set of ethical and moral attributes, as well as an appropriate perspective on the role of the faculty governance unit.

Additional skills for faculty governance unit leaders were oral communication skills, strong organizational ability, strong written communication skills, leadership, educational values, stress tolerance, problem analysis, and sensitivity. These skills relate largely to the perspective that governance body leaders facilitate the process of sharing in decision making, particularly when the governance body is comprised of experts in various disciplines who often have vastly different ideas about defining effective communication.

Governance Leadership Tasks

Organizational behavior dictates a certain degree of shared responsibility, particularly in the areas of separated responsibilities for management. This separation of activities can range from dividing responsibility for paperwork or scheduling, to background research on critical issues being considered. As shown in Table 3, governance leaders had the most agreement on the task of developing data bases for governance decision making. This implies a rationale decision-making process where data sets are utilized in seeking solutions to difficult decisions, and further implies that the governance unit leader is the one most responsible for identifying potential.

Additional tasks for governance leaders include obtaining and allocating resources for the governance unit, developing networks and linkages for the unit, developing a sense of direction for the unit, taking care of the details of running the unit, and developing a sense of pride for the unit.

Table 3.   Tasks of Faculty Governance Unit Leaders (N = 183)

Tasks	Mean Rating	(SD)	Rank
Develop databases for governance decision making	4.47	(1.20)	1
Obtain and allocate resources for the unit	4.06	(1.00)	2
Develop networks and linkages for yourself	4.04	(1.03)	3
Develop a sense of direction for the unit	3.98	(1.10)	4
Take care of details of running the unit	3.98	(.96)	4
Develop a sense of pride for the unit	3.89	(1.32)	6

Career Futures

The relationship between the governance unit leader and college administration often involves the handling of intimate, sensitive information and decision making, and these character-defining interactions can build the bridges necessary for faculty to assume appointments in the college's administration. Trow (1990) distinctly argued that this was not the case, and that faculty tend to get involved in decision making as a result of opposition to administration.

Another framework of thinking about governance unit service is that it provides the experiences and exposure necessary to assume an administrative position through competitive application. This argument holds that experience dealing with individuals from a variety of academic disciplines and working with broad, campus-based issues provides the credentialling necessary for a faculty member to be competitive for different types of administrative positions.

Survey respondents were specifically asked to identify on the survey whether they would consider an administrative position in higher education during the next five years. Of the 180 respondents to the question, 148 (82%) indicated that they would not consider a move into administration. Conversely, this finding does suggest that almost a fifth of all faculty governance leaders do see themselves as future administrators.

DISCUSSION

Faculty participation in governance activities are important both institutionally and individually. Based on the extent of influence and power exerted, faculty groups can forcefully have meaningful impacts on the institution and the entire higher education industry. The academic freedom movement of 30 years ago provides a good example of faculty pressure for institutional change, and reflect a societal interest in retaining and encouraging faculty expertise. Faculty participation, however, has not historically maintained a high enough level of interest and activism to continually support strong levels of influence. Part of the need for examining faculty participation, then, is the need to study, refine, develop, and encourage faculty governance leadership. Despite the marketability of academic leadership development programs by professional associations and institutional continuing education bodies, little authentic change in faculty empowerment has been noted (Birnbaum, 1991).

Leaders surveyed in the NDBFIG project considered themselves to be process oriented and thus, more inclined to expend energy directed at the process of setting up and working with governance procedures rather than taking on meaningful issues that have real consequences to the campus community. Indeed, part of the attractiveness of certain individuals to "leadership" positions in faculty governance may be the structural ability of faculty members to get the work of the body completed. From the perspective of institutional administration, these leaders may well be the most valued, as they facilitate the process of shared decision making without entering truly critical conversations about institutional issues.

In many governance bodies, governance unit leadership is assumed due to the lack of faculty members stepping forward, and based on issues and beliefs, challenge others in getting elected. To some extent, faculty "leadership" is defined by default, for the lack of any other faculty member willing to subject themselves to the process and judgement of others concerning both substantive and procedural issues. Senior administration and fellow faculty members may find these leaders the most difficult to work with, as the lack of a true guiding belief or value system that can be used to clarify decision making.

For some governance bodies, the choice is clarified greatly by the election of a clearly favored and well-liked faculty colleague. These individuals often have the commonsense to provide effective leadership and chose to speak with the collective voice of the entire governance body. These individuals frustrate administration due to their articulate behavior, and draw their success and power from their ability to communicate with the highly specialized and trained faculty of an institution.

So much of faculty cogovernance is reliant on individual performance, entire systems succeed or fail based on the individuals placed in these important roles. The critical leadership discussion that must take place for effective faculty cogovernance to be sustained needs to be based partially on the systematic reform behaviors necessary for meaningful collaboration throughout the institution. The conversation must then be continued based on the foundation of communication channels and how information and voices are shared and channeled throughout the governance body and the institution.

Faculty governance units are exciting bodies when it comes to dealing with institutional issues, but they must overall learn, and learning in this instance is predicated on faculty governance leadership. These individuals have the power to radically transform the direction and nature of the increasingly market driven higher education enterprise, and refocus the important conversation about how to provide higher learning to the nation's population.

REFERENCES

Baldridge, J. V. (1982). Shared governance: A fable about the lost magic kingdom. *Academe, 68*(1), 12-15.

Birnbaum, R. (1988). *How colleges work.* San Francisco: Jossey-Bass.

Birnbaum, R. (Ed.). (1991). The latent organizational functions of the academic senate: Why senates do not work but will not go away. In *Faculty in governance: The role of senates and joint committees in academic decision making. New directions for higher education report 75* (pp. 1-25). San Francisco: Jossey-Bass.

Connick v. Myers, 461 U. S. 137 (1983).

Evans, J. P. (1999). Benefits and barriers to shared authority. In M. T. Miller (Ed.), *Responsive academic decision making involving faculty in higher education governance* (pp. 29-54). Stillwater, OK: New Forums Press.

Floyd, C. E. (1985). *Faculty participation in decision making: Necessity or luxury?* (ASHE-ERIC Higher Education Report No. 8). Washington, DC: Association for the Study Higher Education and ERIC Clearinghouse on Higher Education.

Gilmour, J. E. (1991). Participative governance bodies in higher education: Report of a national study. In R. Birnbaum (Ed.), *Faculty in governance: The role of senates and joint committees in academic decision making. New directions for higher education report 75* (pp. 27-40). San Francisco: Jossey-Bass.

Magney, J. R. (1999). Faculty union organizing on the research campus. *Thought and Action, 15*(1), 111-126.

Miles, A. S. (1997). College law (2nd. ed.). Tuscaloosa, AL: Sevgo Press.

Miller, M. T. (1997). *Faculty governance leaders in higher education: Roles, beliefs, and skills.* Paper presented at the 20th Annual Meeting of the Eastern Educational Research Association, Hilton Head, SC.

Miller, M. T., Garavalia, B. J., & McCormack, T. F. (1996). Community college faculty involvement in governance: Implications for teaching performance. *Michigan Community College Journal, 3*(1), 51-61.

Miller, M. T., & Kang, B. (1999). International dimensions to shared authority in higher education. *Review Journal of Philosophy and Social Science, 24*(1/2), 69-82.

Miller, M. T., McCormack, T. F., Maddox, J., & Seagren, A. T. (1996). Faculty participation in governance at small and large universities: Implications for practice. *Planning and Changing, 27*(3/4), 180-190.

Miller, M. T., & Seagren, A. T. (1993). Faculty leader perceptions of improving participation in higher education governance. *College Student Journal, 27,* 112-118.

Minnesota State Board for Community Colleges v. Knight, 465 U. S. 271 (1984).

Trow, M. (1990). The academic senate. *Liberal Education, 76*(1), 23-27.

Westerfield, R. C. (1997). Personal communication. Tuscaloosa, AL: University of Alabama.

CHAPTER 5

PATH ANALYSIS AND POWER RATING OF COMMUNICATION CHANNELS IN A FACULTY SENATE SETTING

Michael T. Miller
University of Arkansas

Carl Williams
University of Alabama

Brian Garavalia
University of Kansas

Faculty senates and governance units, by design, play a variety of roles in institutional cogovernance. The very nature of defining cogovernance or shared authority can be problematic for these units, as faculty bring a host of expectations to the governance unit, often based on previous experiences and training, administrative allowances, communication patterns, and board involvement in establishing a culture of inclusive decision making. The tenor and tone of inclusive decision making is based both on the rationale for involvement (e.g., legitimate power of the unit) as well as the respect for and authority of decision outcomes.

Policy and University Faculty Governance, 59–73

On the majority of college campuses, Gilmour (1991) argued 90% of all four-year colleges and universities, there is some form of faculty involvement in governance. This involvement may take the form of a faculty senate or council, or in some cases, consists of regularly scheduled town-hall type meetings where all faculty, staff, and administrators gather to consider issues.

The concept of shared governance broadly contends that decision making for the institution is enhanced or somehow made more credible when a variety of constituents are incorporated into the decision-making process. Generally, this means that senior administrators allow front-line employees access to the decision-making process, often on issues related to policy formation or specific issues in need of resolution.

Advocates of shared authority are quick to point out that increased feelings of ownership can create an atmosphere for greater acceptance of decision outcomes, and the act of involving more people in the process allows for the identification of more and more creative solutions to complex problems. Those skeptical of shared authority note the increased time demands necessary to communicate information and data about decisions, a lack of constituent accountability for decisions, and a general feeling of mistrust among faculty and administrators as major barriers to effectively sharing authority.

The result of the skepticism, trust and mistrust, and hope for shared authority has been sporadic research, inconsistent findings on the effectiveness of shared authority, and feelings of doubt as to the worth of the returns on the investment of shared authority efforts. A secondary result on many campuses has been a failure to give notice or reward for those faculty who do commit their energies to involvement. In a sense, shared authority between faculty and administrators is an area that has not progressed in vision or understanding during the past two decades, despite the rapid advances of the academic freedom movement of the early 1970s (Kerr, 1991).

As something of a necessary obligation, relegated to those willing saints who can and will put up with the responsibility, faculty governance units are in a position to justify academic attention. This attention is justified due to the need for involvement by other faculty and administrators, and due to the general accountability issues of higher education. In part responding to the need for academic attention and in part due to the current use and possible abuse of the faculty senate idea, the current study was undertaken to chart the power-related variables of the faculty senate at a major southern research university. Particular attention was directed at the roles of age and gender, as well as communication patterns among faculty senators. The academic year of study was of particular interest due to the system-wide effort to lobby for a state funded pay raise for faculty.

MODELING FACULTY INVOLVEMENT

Faculty governance units continue their existence and functioning on a set of assumptions, whether formalized or not, about why the governance unit exists and produces outcomes. These assumptions generally are informally articulated and passed among generations of faculty through oral traditions and behaviors. Informal and formal mentoring, for example, can provide an arena for the transmission of the traditions of shared authority. These informal traditions have come to be recognized as a series of accepted models for shared governance bodies.

Assumption Set 1:   The Legislative Body

One of the more recent conceptual models for the involvement of faculty in governance to be formalized in the literature has been the conceptualization of a faculty governance unit as serving as a form of legislative branch which must work to hold in check the activities of an executive branch, on a college campus comprised of administrators and administrative units.

The relationship between these two "branches" is then held in check or balanced with what could be considered a judicial branch, that is, the board of directors, governors, or trustees who provide the parameters for the involvement of faculty in different decision-making issues. The board also determines who has the right to do what, what policy can legally be implemented, and finalizes decisions related to the institution, and so forth. On a somewhat responsive basis, a constituent body must bring the issue before the judicial body prior to its taking action. As such, the board serves much like a court where legal action must be taken on legislation passed by congress. Also within this framework is the concept that institutional administrators from the dean or director level through campus chief academic or chief executive officer will influence the behaviors and actions of those serving in a legislative body. For example, deans, vice presidents, provosts, and presidents encourage faculty to embrace something such as research productivity. Nonacademic matters may vary broadly, including an issue of parking policy or whether the administration believes that a campus should be entirely pedestrian. If such a movement comes from the faculty, then the administration is much better situated to act on the matter, develop, and implement the policy to that effect. In so doing, there then arises real questions of ethical power uses by senior administrators. In particular, in working with untenured faculty or in working with faculty on the creation of posttenure review programs. Although this model has not been validated, it does represent a visualization of a campus community driven largely by the competition for scarce resources and political and partisan behavior.

The concept of shared governance, similar to the federal system of the branches of government, is predicated on the belief that individuals want to be involved, and that they will be honest, truthful, and sincere in their dealings. The result in this type of conceptualization is the development and joint reliance on coalition development among faculty subgroups, and the "lobbying" by administrators for faculty support of decision making and policy formation.

Assumption Set 2:   Watch-dog Model

Clark Kerr (1991) contended that faculty members gained the potential to greatly enhance their collective voice in decision making during the turbulence following the academic freedom movement of the late 1960s. He also held that faculty members have largely been reluctant to take advantage of this ability, noting that many faculty have become passive in demanding rights and responsibilities in decision making.

The responsibility of holding administrators accountable to faculty and students alike has resulted in the resurgence of a watch-dog model of faculty involvement. In this scenario, a small, select, and highly motivated group of faculty work to stay informed of administrative behaviors, and alert other faculty and campus based groups of decisions which may negatively effect the perceived "good" of the campus. This small group of faculty may operate independent of formal senates or councils, and has been informally referred to as "faculty radicals."

These "radicals" often find a sense of fulfillment and motivation in their belief that they maintain the integrity and best interests of the campus community. Additionally, the common belief has been that large numbers of faculty prove ineffective in keeping a close watch on administrators, but large groups are believed to be essential in times of crises to maintain some degree of faculty control over administrators.

Assumption Set 3:   Ladder Approach

Faculty involvement, as seen through both the perspective of faculty and administrators, has been classified as a process which allows for the empowerment of faculty members. This empowerment, which can be equated with span of control and responsibility issues, has been conceptualized along the framework of Arnstein's (1976) and Murphy's (1991) work, depicted as a ladder of involvement. Within this model, faculty members are involved to varying degrees based on administrative allowances, where individual administrators and administrative units work through policy and behavior to involve or restrict the involvement of faculty in a host of decision-making episodes.

Arnstein developed a ladder of citizen involvement based on the contention that citizens, namely parents, have a right and responsibility to be involved in local secondary school decision making. Drawing on much of the literature and practical involvement of site-based management and citizen responsibility, Arnstein contended that parents and citizens are involved to varying extents, dependent on the willingness of the local school authority to allow for shared authority.

Arnstein's work was applied to the context of faculty involvement, adapting the "ladder" to reflect the position and environment of higher education (Miller, McCormack, Maddox, & Seagren, 1996). This conceptualization holds that faculty can be entirely restricted (Noninvolvement) in their involvement, resulting in feelings of manipulation (see Table 5.1).

As administrators allow for increased involvement, faculty feelings of ownership may be fluid and flow through levels of therapy, information sharing, and placation. In such a situation, senior administrators may involve faculty to the extent that data and decisions are presented as a matter of information, and may allow for restricted involvement to placate faculty needs in feeling ownership or responsibility for the institution or academic unit.

The characteristics typically identified within each level of involvement tend to have a primarily administrative focus, as indicated by span of control and delegation, in the lower levels of Manipulation (Level 1) and Therapy (Level 2). Higher levels of involvement tend to be more faculty-centered, and offer faculty members the ability to make decisions and

Table 5.1.   Conceptual Ladder of Faculty Involvement in Governance

Level	Degree of Power
8	Faculty control
7	Delegated power
6	Partnership
5	Placation
4	Consultation
3	Informing
2	Therapy
1	Manipulation

function within the collegiate environment. Munn (1996), based on an extensive literature review, defined the characteristics of each level from the standpoint of both administrators and faculty, and concluded that the governance process in higher education is based entirely on the human relations aspects and interpersonal skills of administrators and the faculty who participate in the institution.

Assumption Set 4:   Six Perceptions Model

A team of researchers at the University of Washington conducted an in-depth study of how faculty perceived their role in the governance process and the activities they undertook to be involved or noninvolved (Williams, Gore, Broches, & Lostoski, 1987). By developing a set a statements to be clustered by faculty, the research team identified orientations by which faculty chose to be involved or noninvolved. The orientations, including collegials, activists, acceptors, herarchicals, copers, and the disengaged, were then presented in an overarching orientation of the governance process, where they were further defined by variables of concern for governance issues, confidence in the faculty's governance role, and age.

Presenting this framework in the form of an inverted pyramid, the faculty was comprised of different perceptions of the governance process, and these perceptions often dictate or reflect the willingness of individuals to become involved. The orientations presented include:

- *Collegial*:   Prefer shared governance approach. Oppose collective bargaining. Oppose strong administrative role. Tenured. Two thirds are full professors.
- *Activists*:   Supportive of collective bargaining and other mechanisms for increasing the faculty's governance role, which they view presently as weak. Reject strong administrative role. More approving of traditional collegial mechanisms than Acceptors.
- *Acceptors*:   More accepting of faculty's governance role than the Hierarchials. Willing to go along with what the other's decide. Limited experience in faculty senate. Less concerned than the Copers with women/minority faculty.
- *Hierarchials*:   Prefer strong administrative role. Respond negatively to strong faculty role and to collegial mechanisms now in place. Reject collective bargaining.
- *Copers*:   Middle-range faculty who are managing to "get by." Many associate professors. Light teaching load. Supportive of minority/women faculty colleagues. More supportive of collective bargaining than the Disengaged.

- *Disengaged*: Do not participate in faculty government. Tend to disparage faculty governance role. Oppose collective bargaining. Productive researchers (Williams, Gore, Broches, & Lostoski, 1987, p. 648).

The authors reaffirmed their notation that governance activities can be classified along traditional lines, such as those presented by Robert Birnbaum (1988), yet the process can be more fluid and situational forcing the blurring of these lines. As such, the model draws strength from the contention that faculty involvement is based primarily on how specific issues or topics touch on personal value systems. The response of faculty, then, can be reflective of coalition building and the position or support of administration and fellow colleagues.

Assumption Set 5:   The Godfather

Increasingly on the college campus, the college president plays the role of setting the overall institutional agenda. This agenda, often bartered between the presidential candidate and the selection committee or board of trustees, can be resistant to the evolutionary state of the campus. Rosovsky (1990) noted this phenomenon, as did Bergmann (1991) and others who have claimed that presidential leadership often runs contrary to faculty depiction's of organizational evolution. As the faculty, as a disparate group of constituents, respond to issues, the president or provost assumes a position of control or manipulation over faculty through formal and informal power relationships.

Birnbaum (1988) described different visions of presidential leadership where the position, as much as the person holding the position, relate to faculty and others from a position of manipulation. Much like a "godfather," the institution's president works to control the agenda of the faculty governance unit through intimidation, manipulation, coercion, and office-based power. In some instances, the president's position relies on charismatic leadership to engage faculty constituents, and in others, office-based power is the strategy of choice. Regardless of where the president draws power, the intent of the relationship in this model between the president and the faculty governance unit is one of manipulation and control beyond the normal workings of a traditional political model.

RESEARCH PROCEDURES AND RESULTS

To gain an understanding of the communicative behaviors of the faculty senate participants, observational research techniques were used. These techniques included the rating of each communication episode on a 10-point scoring sheet, which was completed by a team of five graduate students enrolled in a professional education program. Permission to complete the observations was obtained at the last faculty senate meeting of the 1996-1997 academic year, and the rating team observed the nine faculty senate meetings of the 1997-1998 academic year. The observation team was seated in to the side of the senate body and made every effort to not interact with the senators.

The faculty senate being studied was comprised of 62 representatives from 10 academic units (schools and colleges). In addition to these representatives who were full-time, tenure-track faculty, there were representatives from the provost's office and the student government body.

The faculty senate meetings were listed as open to the public, although few individuals without a vested interest in the senate decision making attended. As the purpose for conducting the study was to identify communication channels within the faculty senate, the 10-point scoring sheet was used to code all oral communication encounters by each faculty senator (see Table 5.2).

The first phase of data collection included the creation of a 10-question scoring sheet. These questions related to the communication episode by individual faculty senators. Each verbal communication was scored by a team of raters, with a possible strength of each episode totaling 10. These items, as shown in Table 5.2, assumed that if an oral statement was made independent of a request, and that if the statement either produced or continued a conversation, then the statement had a greater group impact and was subsequently more powerful.

**Table 5.2.   Questions for Determining
Power Channel Communication Scores**

Question	Possible Response (Points)	
1. Was the comment requested?	Y (0)	N (1)
2. Was the comment self-initiated?	Y (1)	N (0)
3. Was it a response?	Y (1)	N (0)
4. Was it followed?	Y (1)	N (0)
5. Was it followed?	Y (1)	N (0)
6. Did the topic die?	Y (0)	N (1)
7. Was it the same theme?	Y (1)	N (0)
8. Was it loud enough for everyone to hear?	Y (1)	N (0)
9. Were the comments/words accepted?	Y (1)	N (0)
10. Questions based on the comments?	Y (1)	N (0)

A three-month summer school term was dedicated to the training of the five-person research team in how to conduct the scoring and in the refining of the scoring form. Several changes were made to the scoring form, primarily directed at making it easier for team raters to complete the 10 questions in a quick and accurate manner.

The first meeting of the year was held in August, and the team of five raters all sat in the back of the meeting room, to the side, so as to mini-mize their presence in the faculty senate meeting. Raters were seated at least 30 minutes before each meeting, so that as faculty senators arrived, they would not be socializing or discussing the project with participants. The observations were not recorded in any other fashion, so the guiding assumption of the data collection was that these raters were accurate and complete in monitoring faculty senate meetings.

A total of nine faculty senate meetings were observed. These meetings lasted from 39 minutes to 90 minutes. The five meeting raters attended all of the meetings. At the end of each meeting, the rating team met with the principal investigator to review the ratings. Any inconsistencies of rat-ings were discussed at length until agreement on the ratings for each item were reached.

Data were sorted by individual faculty senators, although later analysis did provide for some clustering of senator comments. A template of the room was provided to the principal investigator, who cross-referenced seating locations with individual names. Although seat assignments were not mandatory, there was a consistency in seating habits.

For initial analysis, only individuals who had made a minimum of 30 oral statements for each 120-minute period were included. These individ-uals were seated typically in the rear left of the meeting room and from the upper-middle section of the right hand side of the meeting room (for a diagram of the senate meeting room, see Figure 5.1). The mean scores for these groups of individuals were collapsed, and overall directional power ratings for each group were computed.

Power Channels

The group seated in the middle, right side of the senate consisted of a group of vocal individuals. These senators had over 30 communication encounters per 120 minutes in two directions: toward the front of the room (president and secretary) and toward the group of senators from the back left corner of the room (see Figures 5.2 and 5.4). This group in the back left corner similarly communicated at least 30 times with the center right group. The center right group's communication mean scores, for a group of four senators, was 7.28 toward the front and 7.02 toward the rear

1 2	3 4	5 6	A	7 8	9 10	11 12
1 2	3 4	5 6	B	7 8	9 10	11 12
1 2	3 4	5 6	C	7 8	9 10	11 12
1 2	3 4	5 6	D	7 8	9 10	11 12
1 2	3 4	5 6	E	7 8	9 10	11 12
1 2	3 4	5 6	F	7 8	9 10	11 12
1 2	3 4	5 6	G	7 8	9 10	11 12
1 2	3 4	5 6	H	7 8	9 10	11 12

Refreshment Table

Figure 5.1.   The senate line up.

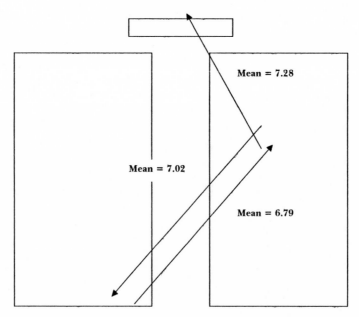

Figure 5.2.   Primary senate communication channels with power ratings (over 30 communication encounters per 120 minutes).

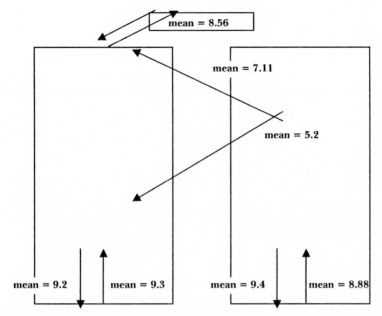

Figure 5.3.   Secondary senate communications channels (under 30 CEs per 120 minutes, minimum of 5 CEs).

of the room, indicating a rather high mean communication rating. The rear group of five senators communication scores were clustered to achieve a mean rating of 6.79 in the direction of the center right group. Thus, the two primary communication channels in the senate were between a group of four senators in the upper-center right side and five senators who consistently sat in the back left rear of the senate meeting room.

Secondary communication channels were those where under 30 communication encounters were observed and noted per 120 minutes (with a minimum of 5 communication encounters; see Figure 5.3). Again, the same four senators provided the most communication encounters, directed at a group in the middle-left of the senate and to the senate leadership (secretary) in the front of the senate meeting room, with an average power rating of 5.2 and 7.11, respectively. Additional channels were noted between senators sitting in the back right side of the room and the back left side of the room, observed as sending and receiving, with means of 9.4 and 8.88 for the right and 9.2 and 9.0 on the left. Senate leadership also communicated within its own group, with a sending power rating of 8.3 from the president to the secretary and 8.56 from the secretary to the president.

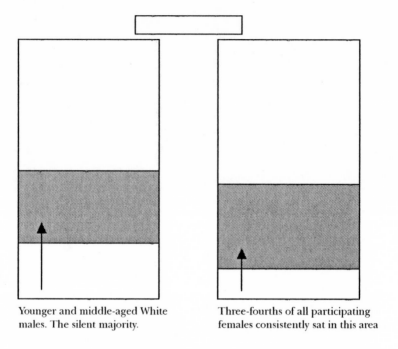

Younger and middle-aged White
males. The silent majority.

Three-fourths of all participating
females consistently sat in this area

Figure 5.4.   Gender distribution patters.

Correlation Indices

The mean power ratings of the communication encounters were correlated to the pass-fail ratios of legislation, resolutions, and motions (see
Figure 5.5). The mean power score correlations identified moderate to
low relationships for the middle right side group at the following levels: .68 for communication encounters with the president, .70 for communication encounters with the senate secretary, .21 for encounters with
a group in the mid-lower left, and .10 for encounters with the rear left
group. The rear left group similarly had a low correlation between
power rating of communication encounter (6.79) and legislation passages, at the .33 level. Conversely, there were strong correlations
between the president and secretary (.89 sending and .90 receiving,
respectively), and for the two internal communication channels in the
rear of the senate meeting room. The rear right group had sending-
receiving correlations of .80 and .84, and the rear left had sending-
receiving correlations of .69 and .72.

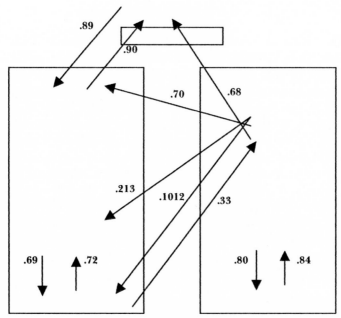

Figure 5.5.   Correlation patterns for CEs and decision making (as defined by passing legislation, resolutions, motions).

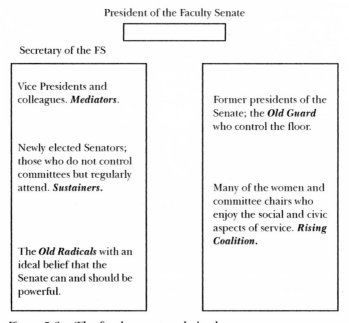

Figure 5.6.   The faculty senate: who's who.

CONCLUSIONS

The findings of the communication channels and correlations provide for the identification of very specific trends in who is participating in the decision-making process for the senate. The group with the most collective input into the decision-making process were generally older, more senior faculty members who had served in leadership roles of the senate, particularly in the role of senate president. In what could be termed the "old guard," these individuals often had comments about their perceptions of university business and governance, and typically controlled the amount of time others could provide commentary (see Figure 5.6). These comments did not sway others in voting, but they did operate as a form of control in their continuous discussion and utilization of time. For these faculty members, the senate could best be seen as an opportunity for placation. Similarly, the activities of the senate could be described as largely political in nature, as coalition development seemed to be common within the two subgroups located at the rear of the senate meeting room. Although the potential did exist for the body to act as a watch-dog group, the group was responsive rather than activist-based, and exhibited many of the characteristics identified by the Williams team in Washington. Also, there was no identification of the role of the college president in the senate, so no clear validation of the godfather assumption set could be extended from study findings. Ironically, this very indication that no role of the president was indicated could be a sign that the president was indeed behaving as a godfather. A more content driven investigation, however, would be needed to determine the point of origin for pieces of legislation and resolutions.

Study findings point to several meaningful conclusions beyond the identification of the old guard and old radicals. Perhaps most obvious is the indication that the behavior of several groups of faculty in a nondirected manner (other than placation) may be a disincentive for others to be involved in a meaningful debate and conversation about issues and ideas. This disincentive may also be a point of discussion in Miller's finding that one of the primary indices of faculty senate leadership participation is an invitation to participation rather than a desire to make the institution a better place through involvement.

Another dimension to this example of involvement is the question of effectiveness and efficiency. The Southern Association of Colleges and Schools, for example, has mandated a broad-based inclusive decision-making process that is effective and efficient. The number of communication encounters and influence of these encounters suggests there is a great deal of noneffective communication. Assuming that the faculty senate is intended to serve as a decision-making body with some authority, then the result is a body which is not efficient. This does, however, suggest that the senate under study may have much more value in its social dimensions, particularly in how faculty senators viewed the informal acculturation process and the social aspects of interacting with other professionals from diverse academic backgrounds.

In addition to a further exploration of these dimensions of the faculty senate, there is a need to examine how the college president interacts with faculty senators and whether this reenforces one of the existing assumption sets or alters the entire view of the governance unit. Detailed study of the rationale for the methods of interaction would also be valuable and instructive in creating an environment where a faculty senate could be more effective in leading policy reformation and representing faculty interests.

REFERENCES

Arnstein, S. A. (1976). A ladder of citizen participation. In E. Ingram & R. McIntosh (Eds.), *Adaptive processes in educational organizations*. Edmonton: University of Alberta.

Bergmann, B. (1991). Bloated administration, blighted campuses. *Academe, 68*(1), 12-15.

Birnbaum, R. (1988). *How colleges work*. San Francisco: Jossey-Bass.

Gilmour, J. E. (1991). Participative governance bodies in higher education: Report of a national study. In R. Birnbaum (Ed.), *Faculty in governance: The role of senates and joint committees in academic decision making. New directions for higher education report 75* (pp. 27-40). San Francisco: Jossey-Bass.

Kerr, C. (1991). *The great transformation in higher education*. Albany, NY: State University of New York.

Miller, M. T., McCormack, T. F., Maddox, J., & Seagren, A. T. (1996). Faculty participation in governance at small and large universities: Implications for practice. *Planning and Changing, 27*(3/4), 180-190.

Munn, B. M. (1996). Shall the university be controlled by the trustees, administrators, or faculty? Unpublished manuscript, The University of Alabama, Tuscaloosa, AL.

Murphy, P. J. (1991). A collaborative approach to professional development. *Education Research and Perspectives, 18*(1), 59-65.

Rosovsky, H. (1990). *The university an owner's manual*. New York: W. W. Norton.

Williams, D., Gore, W., Broches, C., & Lostoski, C. (1987). One faculty's perceptions of its governance role. *Journal of Higher Education, 58*(6), 629-655.

CHAPTER 6

FACULTY GOVERNANCE IN THE ACADEMIC DEPARTMENT

The Role of the Chair

Steve Vacik
Bevill State Community College

In recent years, the role of the department chair has come under both greater professional and scholarly attention. Due in part to growing demands for greater accountability throughout all sectors of higher education, and due in part to the growing scores of specialized administrators (Kerr, 1991), the chair position has become a topic of a growing body of literature (Seagren & Miller, 1995). Additionally, Roach (1976) claimed that up to 80% of all of higher education institutions' decisions are made at the departmental level. This latter concern about where decisions are being made is of the utmost interest to those working in faculty involvement in governance and in particular, those working to keep administrative growth in balance to instructional issues.

The departmental chair position has been described as "caught in the middle" (Seagren & Miller, 1994) between faculty demands and administrative pressures. The ambiguity of reporting lines, then, demands that the chair report to two masters (Creswell, Wheeler, Seagren, Egly, & Beyer, 1990), both faculty, for whom the chair must serve as an advocate, and administrators, who see the chair position as a fulcrum to the imple-

Policy and University Faculty Governance, 75–84
Copyright © 2003 by Information Age Publishing
All rights of reproduction in any form reserved.

mentation of college or institutional policy (Seagren, Creswell, & Wheeler, 1993; Creswell et al., 1990). Indeed, the chair position has typically been identified as existing within a dilemma, where pressures are alternatively placed on the individual from opposite directions (Seagren, Creswell, & Wheeler, 1993; Seagren & Miller, 1994). Miller (1995) conversely argued that the chair position is situated within a web, where various constituencies, including upper level administrators, faculty, students, external advisory groups, and so forth, all have the potential to place a strain on the chair's performance. The middle ground is felt no where more acutely than in issues related to faculty governance. Virtually all curricular decisions are dealt with at some level in the academic department, and the chair must choose a role carefully, one of either promoting possibly administrative-directed changes or policies, or to the contrary, advocating faculty rights to the curriculum.

Miller (1999) argued that the academic department chair is something of an administrative and faculty "whip," responsible for mustering support or action. This contention, of course, is predicated on faculty rights to involvement and an implied leadership ability among faculty. Bennett (1989) argued that the department chair may be the most influential and important administrative position in higher education today. If the estimation proposed by Roach (1976) is still valid, nearly 80% of decisions made in colleges and universities are at the departmental level. This level is divided into academic units or departments, with a chair acting as the head and the body composed of the faculty and support staff (Seagren et al., 1993). The functions of the department have traditionally included academic course design and delivery, scholarly research, and service to the internal and external communities (Bennett, 1983; Bennett & Figuli, 1990). These are the daily decisions which drive the university and cannot be neglected, and thus, the department functions as the principal vehicle for the delivery of services at the university, and the chair, as the head of the department, is involved in making many of the vital decisions on campus (Anderson, 1976; Bennett, 1982; Bennett, 1990; Seedorf & Gmelch, 1989; Seagren et al., 1993). In fact, Peltason (1984) argued that the chair position is so important that, "an institution can run for a long time with an inept president, but not for long with inept chairpersons" (p. xi).

The current discussion is framed around the importance of the chair in fostering or controlling some level of faculty involvement in governance. As such, a discussion of the chair's role and leadership is presented and followed with highlights of how this highly important position intersects with faculty governance.

DEPARTMENT CHAIR ROLES

Johnson (1988) reported that Bakersfield College recently examined the role of the department chair as perceived by the faculty, administration, and chairs. The study determined that department chairs were "caught in the middle" between the expectations of the faculty, which included scheduling of classes and the communication of the needs to the college, and the administration, which included leadership, evaluation of faculty, motivation of faculty and increased productivity. To underscore the dilemma faced by the chair, Johnson reprinted a speech he gave to his department. In his speech, Johnson reiterated that he had a responsibility both to the faculty and to the administration. In order to prepare the department for coming changes, he assumed many of the characteristics expected by the administration, such as leadership, motivation, and increased productivity, while at the same time attempting to meet the expectations of the faculty.

The Center for the Study of the Department Chair (1990) conducted a national survey which dealt with job satisfaction levels among department chairs. Most chairs indicated that they were rarely satisfied with their respective job responsibilities, with approximately 2% indicating that they were satisfied most of the time with their positions. Responses from the chairs who received general satisfaction from their positions were divided into three categories: personal, altruistic, and vicarious. Those chairs that fell in the personal category experienced satisfaction when they were personally able to achieve success while serving as chair, such as in finding time to complete personal research along with their daily administrative duties. The altruistic chairs received satisfaction when they were able to help students and faculty for the good of the department, such as in hiring qualified faculty members or making improvements for the good of the department. Finally, the vicarious chairs expressed satisfaction when others in their department made significant achievements, such as faculty producing quality research or students finding employment upon graduation. Those chairs dissatisfied with their roles reflected the idea that circumstances beyond their control, such as too much paperwork or unsupportive higher administration, caused obstacles which impeded goal attainment.

Goldenberg (1990) reported on her fears and concerns corresponding to her selection and appointment as department chair in a two-year college. She found that the position was ambiguous and lacked a defined role and duties. Rather than the true "boss," an expectation often thrust on a department chair, she found herself as a "first among equals," a position she personally did not find conducive to the tasks she faced as department chair.

Seagren et al. (1993) found that the role of the chair hinged on three specific elements: communication, decision making, and issues of authority. First, chairs serve as the most important link in the communication chain at most colleges and universities. They oversee the daily activities of the department, and are called on to deal with the senior level administration, faculty, and students and keep the lines of communication flowing from one group to the next (Weinberg, 1984; Seagren & Miller, 1995). Second, chairs are called on to make the important decisions affecting students, faculty, and support staff (Fife, 1982). Finally, the authority invested in academic chairs extends over issues of greatest importance to the departmental constituents (Bennett 1982; Gmelch & Carroll, 1991; Carroll & Gmelch, 1992).

Carroll and Gmelch (1992) found that chairs, in assessing their roles, view activities which directly benefit their department as more important than ones which are perceived as college-wide. Of primary importance to highly-effective chairs are those duties which directly assist their faculty colleagues. Also, in self-reporting their duties, highly-effective department chairs listed those duties as most important which they believed they accomplished most successfully. Chairs were grouped, according to their roles, into four groups: leader chairs, scholar chairs, developer chairs, and manager chairs. The importance placed on a specific duty determined the role a chair would perform in carrying out the position. For example, leader chairs saw their most important duty as representing the department to the university, while scholar chairs gave greater importance to remaining current within an academic discipline than did all other groups.

Miller, Benton, and Vacik (1998) examined the role of the department chair in the two-year colleges as fiscal managers. They found that, with the expanded mission and growth of community colleges, certain strategies among mid-level administrators were consistently utilized in dealing with budgetary reductions while maintaining (or enhancing) program quality. The results from their three-round Delphi survey determined that effective resource management strategies included addressing issues of human resource management jointly with fiscal issues and relying more heavily on planning at the departmental rather than the college level.

CHAIRS AS LEADERS

The basic assumption in studying the department chair is that the position is based on leadership ability. Bennett (1989) draws on his experience with academic chairs in defining four leadership styles among chairs and the subsequent effects on their department. The four types of chairs are hopefuls, survivors, transients, and adversaries. Hopefuls are often relatively new to the position and they believe that their leadership can make a difference in the department. These chairs are often happy to have been selected to the position and seek ways to empower individual faculty members. Survivors have an entirely different style, according to Bennett, predicated on having served as chair for 10 years or more. Some survivors are invaluable to the institution, as they present stability and perspective to the department; other survivors are simply "caretakers" (p. 10) and need to be replaced. Transients are most common in institutions where the department chair is an elected, rotating position. Transients most often are hesitant to take the position and do so only for the least amount of time required by departmental custom. This leadership style is uninspired and provides little benefit to the department or the faculty member "forced" into the position. Adversarials are angry chairs who perceive policy changes as direct challenges to their authority. They generally serve as the foil for hopeful chairs, often portraying issues in the worst possible manner. Bennett concludes that more hopeful chairs are needed and that the chair position requires constant review to maintain its vitality.

Leadership effectiveness is predicated on style, which varies from individual chair to individual chair (Seagren, Creswell, & Wheeler, 1993). Also, leadership requirements for the chair may differ:

> according to a department's current place in its cycle of overall development and its relation to the model of governance at a particular institution (Seagren, Creswell & Wheeler, 1993, p. 22).

The successful chair (leader) must have vision, have access to necessary information via databases, and an understanding of the politics inherent in higher education (Bennett, 1989; Creswell et al., 1990; Seagren, Creswell & Wheeler, 1993).

The transition and development from faculty member to academic chair is a difficult process and one which has generated many recent studies. Petrash (1988) determined that relatively few chairs were prepared to accept their current positions. They did not understand how their jobs would change from instructor to administrator, nor did they have the training to serve as a successful administrator. Petrash found that chairs needed training in three basic areas: managing people, managing time, and managing the self. In managing people, the most important principle according to the author is that the new chair must become "coach," instead of "star," in order to inspire colleagues to work together as a team. Managing time successfully requires proper prioritization of tasks and duties, with special attention given to budgetary matters. Petrash also resolved that managing the self is a key component to development as a chair, with an emphasis on professional development opportunities and involvement with colleagues at other institutions, through professional and state associations.

Seedorf (1991) examined the encounter stage (the first stage) in the promotion of a faculty member to chair as the most important. Her study examined the satisfaction levels, time management issues, and personal adjustment to the position. The finding was that, although most chairs were initially satisfied with their new positions, they had markedly less time for other aspects of their lives.

Litterest (1993) similarly found that in order to maximize their creativity necessary to perform well, chairs needed to see their jobs as positive challenges and opportunities. To that end, they have required the assistance of higher administration to help remove blocks, such as lack of time and overresponsibility, to unleash their creative abilities.

CHAIRS INTERSECTING WITH FACULTY GOVERNANCE

The overriding concern that chairs must consider is a personal declaration of what is expected from an academic democracy, and to what extent that democratic expectation has rights and responsibilities. Most chairs succumb to faculty decision making related to curricular concerns and student issues, such as admissions, but provide only information related to staff supervision and evaluation, budget management, facilities control, and so forth. Indeed, a substantial component of departmental management relates to nonacademic matters, and many chairs simply provide faculty with information on what they may personally deem to be a "need-to-know" basis.

As Miller (1999) argued, though, faculty involvement in governance relates to much more than departmental politics and decision making at the lowest possibly level. The department chair can play a pivotal role in getting faculty to participate in institutional governance. The difficulty, as noted in the rather abundant chair literature, is that there is little to no mention or concern about how chairs build departments that value decision making. Being a "good" chair becomes a subjective definition based on an institution's satisfaction with performance in often unrelated areas (for example, faculty evaluation and office equipment maintenance contract review). Chairs, conversely, seem to get into trouble when they alienate faculty or make decisions without departmental support, and the result is either encouragement from a dean's office (in the case of forcing change on a department) or the removal of the chair. The consistency in performance for chairs must come, therefore, from a set of beliefs and values about education and faculty rights. The Seagren (1994) team alluded to this in their study of community college department chairs, but they did not explore what that might really mean and what kind of impact that can have on an entire institution and beliefs about social justice.

Dill and Helm (1988) have argued that the types of decisions being placed before faculty governance bodies has changed from maintenance type decisions, like those typically made by a department chair, to strategic policy decisions. Additionally, as Eckel (2000) contends, faculty governance is responsive and reliant on the types of issues being presented to either enlist or disengage potential faculty participation. The role of the chair, then, does evolve into one of a political whip. If 80% of all institutional decisions are indeed made at the departmental level, then the chair position becomes perhaps the most important and critical in framing how faculty governance is implemented and essentially defined. When chairs believe in the value of shared governance, they create the environment and culture for sharing in decision making. Although they may not have the power to stop faculty when an issue strikes particularly close to heart, they do have the ability to muster support for any variety of issues that can potentially impact an individual department. In such an environment, academic colleges can then evolve into centers of power, based not on traditional definitions of reputation and finances, but on ideals, influence, articulation, and democratic ideals.

Chairs, in such a vital role, must consider how and whether they value academic democracy. If they do embrace the basic idea that the college culture and experience for students is better by responsibly sharing authority, then a set of strategies need to be developed to enable this to happen. These, in essence, are points of opportunity for department chairs. As all institutions differ and have different sets of cultural boundaries, this listing is only a basic guide to initiate strategic conversations about building an academic democracy.

1. Provide a departmental reward structure that recognizes involvement. The reward does not have to be fiscal compensation for involvement, but can and should involve public recognition and gratitude for service. Many departments can also provide service credit for involvement with governance activities, and chairs need to be leaders in helping faculty figure out how to structure a presentation of this service.

2. Create an expectation of communication from those providing representation. Chairs should be in a position to expect faculty representatives to report on their work and the work of the larger governance body. Chairs need to allow time at departmental meetings to discuss governance issues, and to recognize the leadership

role that the representative is taking on. This also serves a dual purpose in developing other faculty leaders.

3. Define consistent expectations of governance between the department, the academic college, and the institution at large. Inconsistencies can be confusing and perplexing for faculty and for program assessment. Chairs need to work hard to align departmental expectations for involvement in governance with the expectation in the college as a whole. These expectations similarly need to reflect an institutional-wide philosophy for shared governance.

4. Build an environment that breeds future representation and builds a sense of expectation for involvement that can transcend faculty generational issues. One of the most common barriers to shared governance involvement is the notion that older generations of faculty dominate conversations and issues. Chairs can be important conduits for changing this culture and can use their own authority to develop teams of faculty to study and make recommendations on key issues. Team work, as a management philosophy, needs to be part of the department chair's tool box of administrative skills, and chairs need to exercise this strategy in building feelings of responsibility and responsiveness.

5. Provide the leadership necessary to get faculty involvement and buy-in, and invest in the shared governance process. This means that chairs can not make decisions in a vacuum, and must rely in and trust a system of shared authority. Similarly, chairs need to demonstrate in their actions that sharing authority is important and is valued in the daily life of the department.

6. Find a way to assess shared governance and let faculty know whether or not it is working. Speculation by some can introduce negative energy into the creation of a shared governance environment, and chairs must be able to demonstrate in a meaningful way that shared governance is or is not working. If it is not working, then chairs need to be the first in line to reconceptualize how a system might work better. Creative mechanisms such as governance portfolios including issues addressed, voting behaviors/patterns, recommendations, and so forth, can be one highly effective evaluation method.

Higher education is at an important point in its historical development. For the first time institutions are being seriously challenged by for-profit providers, including the on-line industry and corporate universities, and institutions need to find ways to demonstrate a value-added experience. A big part of that value-added experience is the holistic intellectual development of individuals, and faculty need to be empowered to find ways to make that happen. Faculty members, who comprise the majority of institutional payrolls, need to be involved in meaningful ways in institutional life, and the academic department chair is the leading voice in making that involvement happen.

REFERENCES

Anderson, G. L. (1976). Organizational diversity. In J. C. Smart & J. R. Montgomery (Eds.), *Examining departmental management*. New Directions for Institutional Research No. 2. San Francisco: Jossey-Bass.

Bennett, J. B. (1982). Inside a department chairperson. *AGB Reports, 24*(3), 39-42.

Bennett, J. B. (1983). *Managing the academic department.* New York: Ace/Macmillan.

Bennett, J. B. (1989). About department chairs. *AAHE Bulletin, 42*(2), 9-11.

Bennett, J. B. (1990). The dean and the department chair: Toward greater collaboration. *Educational Record, 71*(1), 24-26.

Bennett, J. B., & Figuli, D. J. (Eds.). (1990). *Enhancing departmental leadership: The roles of the chairperson.* New York: Ace/MacMillan.

Carroll, J. B., & Gmelch, W. H. (1992). *The relationship of department chair roles to importance of chair duties.* Paper presented at the annual meeting of the Association for the Study of Higher Education, Minneapolis, MN. (ERIC Document Reproduction Service No. ED 352 910).

Center for the Study of Department Chair. (1990). Job satisfaction for chairs. *CSDC Newsletter, 2*(1), 1-3.

Creswell, J. W., Wheeler, D. W., Seagren, A. T., Egly, N. J., & Beyer, K. D. (1990). *The academic chairperson's handbook.* Lincoln, NE: University of Nebraska Press.

Dill, D. D., & Helm, K. P. (1988). Faculty participation in strategic policy making. In J. Smart (Ed.), *Higher education: Handbook of theory and research* (Vol. 4, pp. 319-354). New York: Agathon.

Eckel, P. D. (2000). The role of shared governance in institutional hard decisions: Enabler or antagonist? *Review of Higher Education, 24*, 15-39.

Fife, J. (1982). Foreword. In D. B. Booth (Ed.), *The department chair: Professional development and role conflict. AAHE-Eric Higher Education Research Report No. 10.* (ERIC Document Reproduction Service No. ED 226 689).

Gmelch, W. H., & Carroll, J. B. (1991). The three Rs of conflict management for department chairs and faculty. *Innovative Higher Education, 16*, 107-123.

Goldenberg, M. (1990). Common and uncommon concerns: The complex role of the community college department chair. In J. B. Bennett & D. J. Figuli (Eds.), *Enhancing departmental leadership: The role of the chairperson* (pp. 16-22). New York: McMillan.

Johnson, W. (1988). The role of the department chair. *Innovation Abstracts, 10*(19), 1-2.

Kerr, C. (1991). *The great transformation in higher education.* Albany: SUNY Press.

Litterest, J. K. (1993). *Creativity and the department chairperson: Challenge or oxymoron?* Paper presented at the joint meeting of the Southern States Communication Association and the Central States Communication Association, Lexington, KY.

Miller, M. T. (1995). Administrator opinions of budgeting and fundraising formula use in community colleges. *Community College Journal of Research and Practice, 19*, 109-115.

Miller, M. T. (1999). The department chair as speaker of the house: Shared authority in the community college department. *Community College Journal of Research and Practice, 23*, 739-746.

Miller, M. T., Benton, C., & Vacik, S. M. (1998). Managing scarce resources in the community college: Strategies for the department chair. *Community College Journal of Research and Practice, 22*, 203-212.

Peltason, J. W. (1984). Foreword. In A. Tucker (Ed.), *Chairing the academic department: Leadership among peers.* New York: Ace/MacMillan.

Petrash, D. L. (1988). The instructor as division chair: Surviving the change to administration. *Innovation Abstracts, 10*(26), 1-2.

Roach, J. H. L. (1976). The academic department chairperson: Roles and responsibilities. *Educational Record, 57*(1), 13-23.

Seagren, A. T., Creswell, J. W., & Wheeler, D. W. (1993). *The department chair: New roles, responsibilities and challenges.* ASHE-ERIC Higher Education Report No. 1. Washington: The George Washington University, School of Education and Human Development.

Seagren, A. T., & Miller, M. T. (1994). Caught in the middle: The pressure of chairing the academic unit. *The Department Chair, 1*(1), 2-3.

Seagren, A. T., & Miller, M. T. (1995). Providing student services in the community college department: The chair's role. *Michigan Community College Journal, 1*(2), 59-66.

Seedorf, R. G. (1991). *The transition of the university department chair: What must be left behind?* Paper presented at the annual convention of the American Educational Research Association, Chicago, IL.

Seedorf, R. G., & Gmelch, W. H. (1989). The department chair: A descriptive study. Paper presented at the annual meeting of the American Educational Research Association, San Francisco, CA. (ERIC Document Reproduction Service No. ED 309 713)

Weinberg, S. S. (1984). The perceived responsibilities of the department chairperson: A note of a preliminary study. *Higher Education, 13*, 301-303.

CHAPTER 7

THE RELATIONSHIP BETWEEN FACULTY AND ACADEMIC ADMINISTRATION IN GOVERNANCE FUNCTIONS

Kenneth W. Borland
East Stroudsburg University

INTRODUCTION

It is ironic that in an era when one might expect scholars and leaders to value and accept diversity of cultures, ideologies, opinions, approaches to problem solving and creativity that the relationship between faculty and academic administration in governance functions often fails to model that ideal. In reality, to lesser or greater extents, in most American higher education institutions there remains a dualistic pattern of governance that falls short of the valuing and acceptance of diversity: the "We/They" relationship. It is a pattern which remains antithetical to what Plante (1989, p. 137) identified as a need to, "out of necessity," create "new forms of governance."

What strong influences enforce the We/They relationship between faculty and academic administration in governance functions? What campus dialogue topics and strategies might lead to improvements in the rela-

Policy and University Faculty Governance, 85–94
Copyright © 2003 by Information Age Publishing

tionship between faculty and academic administration? In this chapter both questions are considered.

While no list could be exhaustive, several noteworthy influences on the relationship between faculty and academic administration in governance functions are discussed below. The age of administration, a lack of trust, a difference in tenure, charge differences, and juxtaposed cultures are also discussed in terms of critical conversations and strategies to positively influence shared governance functions.

INFLUENCE

The Age of Administration

Consider the age in which the modern American university emerged and how it influenced the establishment of the We/They relationship. Academic administration, beyond the positioning of a strong president, grew and quickly became embedded and commonplace in higher education early in the first half of the twentieth century. As institutions grew, the detailed work of managing the multiple facets of university education became necessary. The expansion and creation of disciplines and new curricula, the rise of science and research (both its capacity and economy), and professional education, the expansion of student bodies reflecting widened access for women and some minorities, and so forth, necessitated a change in the way university faculty managed their work. Someone from the faculty had to administer, manage, and offer guidance and leadership to this new kind of institution. Naturally, a respected and trusted peer of senior rank from within the university was "tapped" to become the "first among peers" to offer this service.

But in the last half of the twentieth century academic administrators were less often recruited from within the university and more often new to the institution. They arrived on campus knowing little of the shared history, culture, and vision of their new institution's faculty. As universities grew in size, the new work of academic administration became less that of championing a shared faculty vision that was collegially generated. Rather, the work was more bureaucratic and political in its outlook and function. This may have been a necessary approach as institutions grew in size and the number of facets in each multiplied. Faculty had multiple agendas, they less frequently agreed on mission and curriculum, and often had to compete for resources. As the collegiality among faculty and academic administration ebbed away in institutions that were becoming more bureaucratic, political, and even anarchical (which may have shifted academic administration toward brokering for all and championing for the few or even themselves), it is no wonder that the collegiality between faculty and academic administrators, once perceived as "first among equals," began to slip away and the dualistic We/They was enforced (see Veysey, 1965, Geiger, 1986; 1993, Martin, Samels, & Associates, 1997; Birnbaum, 1988.)

A Lack of Trust

Fundamental to every constructive relationship is trust. The more there is a mutual and high level of trust in the relationship between faculty and academic administration in governance functions, the more collegial and productive it can be even if the environment is at times political, bureaucratic, and anarchical. Conversely, when there are lower levels of trust the We/They relationship is enforced. So, what enforces lower levels of mutual trust between faculty and academic administration in governance functions?

Trust is not an automatic: Trust must be earned both by faculty and by academic administration. The academic administration search process is not enough to establish mutual and high levels of trust. Although the candidate for academic administration and the searching faculty will have developed a level of respect for each other, based on dossiers, references, and first impressions, trust is not automatic. Trust, beyond this initial level of respect, must be earned and the earning of trust is often predicated on early and frequent demonstrations of being trustworthy.

Trust and mistrust issues related to governance are not confined to union or nonunion campuses. While the history of the labor movement is richly illustrated with stories of mistrust between management and labor, there are unionized campuses where academic administration trusts faculty and faculty trust academic administration. This mutual trusting may be more or less difficult to establish if the collective bargaining agreement is more "industrial" than "professional" in its essence. No matter the essence of the agreement, for trust to be established both parties must be prepared to meet the letter of the agreement while trying to analyze, interpret, and implement the agreement based on the spirit of the agreement.

"Process" is a critical factor when attempting to build trust between faculty and academic administration. Academic administrators need to quickly understand the traditional informal processes of governance on campus as well as the formal processes. In a study by Miller, McCormack, Maddox, and Seagren (1996, p. 188) faculty responses were noted as suggesting an ideal "process or protocol where faculty are listened to, trusted, and respected for their involvement and contribution." Faculty wish to be trusted and wish to find academic administration trustworthy in regard to their word and the process.

Process can be as or more important than product when it comes to shared governance. To act when faculty are not on campus, to foreshorten dialogue, to skip a step in the process, to withhold information, and so forth, *even for the common good*, can reduce levels of trust between faculty and academic administration. It is important to establish and maintain as thorough a process as is possible or We/They will be enforced.

A Difference in Tenure

In today's colleges and universities, there is a difference in the tenure of faculty and academic administration that influences the We/They relationship. As the adage "in order to move up one must move out" becomes more engrained in American higher education, fewer faculty and mid-level academic administration members will be promoted to the senior academic administration levels within the institutions where they were first members of the faculty. The senior academic administration increasingly comes to the institution from outside faculty and administration experiences. They may have vision for their new institution, but have a relatively shallow or new passion for and intimate knowledge of it. They have not taught beside the faculty, been part of their struggle to bring the institution to its present heights or suffered through the pressures that have brought it into and out of periods of depression. The new academic administration members are, for the most part, outsiders who now want to take up the charge placed on them to lead the institution.

Faculty leaders often have long histories within their institutions. They have spent a great deal of their careers investing in and nurturing the students, programs, and direction of the institution. They know the institution inside and out, its good and its bad, embody its values and are the current bridge back to its heritage and into its future. They have noted the arrival and departure of many in academic administrations along with most of the intangibles of their visions. While the brick and mortar of the administrations' visions remain more obvious long after academic administration personnel changes, the ideals, policies and procedures, programs, and even the names of the academic administration fade into anonymity or become footnotes in institutional histories. Meanwhile, long-term faculty members remain in the memory of alumni and remain on campus to carry the mantle of the institution into the future. It is no wonder that as faculty insist "on their believed 'right' to involvement in governance … (and) believed it was their duty to convince or persuade administrators to see the collective faculty 'voice' as something of value in decision making" (Miller et al., 1996, p. 187).

In the cases where long-term faculty serve under the leadership and share in the governance of long-term academic administration, one would expect that the We/They would be less influential. However, most academic administrations come from outside the campus and stay for relatively brief periods of time. Presidents average seven-year tenures and provosts tend to quickly "move up" into presidencies that are often outside of the institution. The difference in tenure, particularly the relatively short academic administration tenures, influences the We/They.

Charge Differences

Related to the tenure difference that influences the We/They relationship is the difference in charge received by faculty and academic administration. When the faculty receive and fulfill their charge to teach, research, and serve, these actions contribute to the academic administration meeting its charge. Academic administration is typically given a charge to lead all members of the campus toward meeting and exceeding the mission specific and implied collegial, political, and bureaucratic expectations related to the educational and human development of students, enrollment and fiscal management, the harmonious and positive interaction of the campus community within and beyond its boundaries, and other goals. When the academic administration fulfills its charge, the work of the faculty to fulfill its charge should be enhanced.

When every party carries out their charge, the We/They may not be so obvious. Yet, these two charges frequently are not promoted as being so intimately related. Faculty work and academic administration work is often seen, at best, as distantly and indirectly related. A lack of frequent dialogue and common understanding of the symbiotic nature of faculty and academic administration charges can enforce the We/They relationship.

There is another "Charge" related factor that does influence the We/They relationship between faculty and academic administration. In both the public and private sectors of American higher education, academic administration at all levels must serve those for whom they are responsible and must report to the individuals and bodies that give them their charge. The faculty chair of a program is not only charged to serve her or his faculty and students, but the chair must report to the faculty *and* a department head or dean. This is true for the dean and the chief academic officer. These now charges often relate to the making of strategic policy (Eckel, 2000, p. 16). Campus presidents, institution boards, system or denominational officers and boards, and governmental bodies charge academic administration with tasks and responsibilities that do not always contribute to individual or collective faculty agenda. They may be charges that will better serve other constituents. When such charges are given, the We/They of faculty and academic administration in governance functions may be influenced.

The Learning Culture

There is an ongoing cultural shift in American higher education that will influence the We/They relationship between faculty and academic administration in terms of governance functions. It is, perhaps, best described by R. Eugene Rice (2002), Scholar in Residence, Forum on Faculty Roles and Rewards, American Association for Higher Education. He addresses what for faculty was traditionally and predominantly remains a "collegial culture" driven by a "prestige economy." In the last half of the twentieth century this culture was juxtaposed by what was and remains for academic administration a "managerial culture" driven by a "market economy." Some of Rice's characteristics for these two cultures are listed below.

Collegial Culture: Prestige Economy	Managerial Culture: Market Economy
Liberal Arts	Corporate Sector
Research University	Bottom Line
Faculty-oriented	Accountability
Peer Reviewt	Efficiency
Peer Leadership	Productivity
Community of Scholars	Technical Leadership
Tenure	Quantitative
Academic Freedom	Hierarchical
Shared Governance	Customer-Oriented
Qualitative	JudgmentsWorth
Merit	

The differences between these cultures, as described by Rice, have tremendous influence on the We/They relationship. In fact, they serve to enforce it. Consider several issues. In terms of leadership, the Managerial Culture enforces a manager-employee relationship, authority rests within academic administration while responsibility to produce rests within the faculty, the institution has more ownership than the faculty, and "top-down" is implied if not required.

How administrators treat faculty shapes the ways in which faculty react within the governance arena. When administrators act in ways consistent with trusting faculty and appreciating their special knowledge and perspectives, these cases suggest that faculty will play active and complementary roles in governance. (Furthermore,) Administrators must acknowledge their own roles as participants in the shared governance process (Eckel, 2000, p. 34).

As a solution, Rice offers a third culture, a "Collaborative Culture" that is characteristically a "learning organization." It is "bi-cultural" and its work is to create a future. It exercises "generative communication" and is proactive. "Interdependent" and "systemically-oriented" describe this organization. It is "learning centered" in terms of its outcomes and in terms of its relationships and processes. There is not much tolerance for We/They in the Collaborative Culture.

Summary

While no list could be exhaustive, these five noteworthy influences on the relationship between faculty and academic administration in governance functions give us much to which we must respond. The age of administration, a lack of trust, a difference in tenure, charge differences, and juxtaposed cultures influence the too often problematic We/They relationship that continues to exist on college and university campuses. In the following section, critical conversations and strategies beyond those suggested above will be presented.

CRITICAL CONVERSATIONS AND STRATEGIES

If faculty and academic administration wish to improve upon the We/They relationship, a variety of focused, critical conversations must take place on campus. In addition to those suggested in the previous section of this chapter, three critical conversations and related strategies are presented below: productivity, planning, and culture.

Productivity

One of the most pressing issues on American campuses is that of productivity. Whether spoken of in terms of accountability, assessment, retention, program review, posttenure review and those that precede it, audits, and so forth, accountability is an issue about which faculty and academic administrators must converse.

For many faculty and academic administration members, these are new policies, working conditions, processes, and even concepts. While some in the faculty and some within academic administration are becoming expert on these topics, the vast majority are novices. Therefore, before a critical productivity conversation can occur on campus a strategy needs to be implemented that will commonly develop faculty and academic administrators' productivity knowledge base.

The development plan must be crafted to involve both faculty and academic administration in a shared, common program. This program should yield a common knowledge base on which to further productivity dialogue and practice. The source(s) of productivity demands, a glossary of terms, a code of ethical practice, a toolbox of practices, policies and procedures, and the like should be part of that knowledge base. Then, a campus productivity dialogue can be initiated and sustained in order to refine and implement productivity efforts at a higher level of trust, a better understanding of everyone owning these responsibilities rather than a short-term academic administrator, a sharing of the charge, and the ability for everyone to learn and improve through these processes.

Planning

A second issue that certainly comes to bear on governance functions and begs for a critical campus dialogue between faculty and academic administration is planning. Once productivity measures have been taken, the faculty and academic administration are obligated to make decisions and decisions prompt plans to celebrate or plans to change in order to improve. While decision making may be difficult, planning to improve may be even more difficult. Why? First, faculty and academic administration are both heavily invested. Plans impact on values, priorities, policies, procedures, resources, and so forth. No matter what plan emerges from within the faculty or the academic administration, all parties stand to gain, lose, or both. Planning, therefore, can contribute to the We/They relationship in governance functions that lead to decisions and plans. That is, unless the resulting plans have a high level of agreement or "buy-in" from faculty and academic administration.

The best way to approach decision making and the resultant planning is to ensure that there is adequate quantitative and qualitative data, preparation and reflection time (regarding values, structures, processes, resources, etc.) for individuals and units and the institution, as representative and/or widespread participation as is feasible, and appropriate response to the various perspectives that will be voiced. This is an opportunity to demonstrate trust and trustworthiness, commit to the big picture and long-term interest of the institution and its units, explain the context and perspective of all internal and external stakeholders, and to learn what your institution is and really wants to be.

Culture

While a dialogue about the culture of the institution may not at first appear to be critical, it can be very productive. While it may be easy for academic administration and faculty to describe the culture of the campus using Burnbaum's, Rice's, or another's terminology, it is likely that there will be differences of description based on individual and unit experiences (positive and negative) and/or preferences. This dialogue can lead to a better description of what is, but it can then lead to a description of what is desired.

To change a campus culture requires the involvement and cooperation of faculty and academic administration. The dialogue will shape the ideal by raising the questions, "What are we now?" and "What do we need to be and wish to be?" and "Where are the differences and what do we wish to do about them?" If there is no desire to change, as a result of the dialogue the existing culture will be better understood and appreciated. If there is a desire to change, the dialogue will address possible change processes and how decision-making and planning will be done as well as possible new forms of governing. The influences of trust, tenure, and charge must be resolved and then consistently practiced in order to bring about mutually agreed upon, positive, desired cultural change.

CONCLUSION

In most American higher education institutions there remains a dualistic pattern of governance that falls short of the valuing and acceptance of diversity: the We/They relationship between faculty and academic administration in governance functions. It is a pattern that remains antithetical to what Plante (1989, p. 137) identified as a need to, "out of necessity," create "new forms of governance."

In this chapter the strong influences that enforce the We/They relationship and critical campus dialogues and strategies to improve or provide for new relationships were presented. The influences of the age of administration, a lack of trust, a difference in tenure, charge differences, and juxtaposed cultures are ones that can be addressed in order to reduce the

We/They relationship and to provide for improved relationships between faculty and academic administration in governance functions.

REFERENCES

Birnbaum, R. (1988). *How colleges work: The cybernetics of academic organization and leadership*. San Francisco: Jossey-Bass.

Eckel, P. D. (2000). The role of shared governance in institutional hard decisions: Enabler or antagonist? *The Review of Higher Education, 24*(1), 15-39.

Geiger, R. L. (1986). *To advance knowledge: The growth of research universities, 1900-1940*. Oxford: Oxford University Press.

Geiger, R. L. (1993) *Research and relevant knowledge: American research universities since World War II*. Oxford: Oxford University Press.

Martin, J., Samels, J. E., & Associates (1997). *First among equals: The role of the chief academic officer*. Baltimore: The Johns Hopkins University Press.

Miller, M. T, McCormack, T. F., Maddox, J. F., & Seagren, A. T. (1996). Faculty participation in governance at small and large universities: Implications for practice. *Planning and Changing, 27*(3/4), 180-190.

Plante, P. R. (1989). The role of faculty in campus governance. In J. H. Schuster, L. H. Miller, & Associates (Eds.), *Governing tomorrow's campus: Perspectives and agendas* (pp. 116-140). New York: American Council on Education, Macmillan.

Rice, R. E. (2002, March). *Reward systems for integrating outcomes: The path to commitment*. Campus Leadership for Learning Outcomes, Assessment, and Improvement: A Conference for Chief Academic Officers Implementing Characteristics 2002. Middle States Commission on Higher Education. Philadelphia, PA.

Veysey, L. R. (1965). *The emergence of the American university*. Chicago: University of Chicago Press.

PART III

GOVERNANCE ISSUES AND TRENDS

CHAPTER 8

ACADEMIC GOVERNANCE AND FICTION

Ethan Heinen and Julie A. Caplow
University of Missouri–Columbia

INTRODUCTION

In this chapter, we will be viewing faculty governance in higher education through a unique lens—the "college novel." The study of college novels provides an approach by which issues of governance in higher education may be explored. Milan Kundera, (1988) in *The Art of the Novel* suggested that novels provide alternative and effective ways of exploring many types of philosophical questions. In this respect, we consider the novel a useful lens by which to uncover some of the complexities inherent in faculty decision making and governance.

The college novels examined for this chapter were ones in which the major story line is set in a college or university with specific elements of the novel related to faculty governance. Although there are numerous college novels that take place within a higher education setting, the degree to which they actually focus on the workings of the institution may vary considerably. For example, *This Side of Paradise*, by F. Scott Fitzgerald (1920), is set in Princeton University; however, this setting is used only as vehicle for a young man's romance and other personal issues. In this example, the institution and its operations are inconsequential. In con-

Policy and University Faculty Governance, 97–117
Copyright © 2003 by Information Age Publishing

trast, *A Tenured Professor*, by John Kenneth Galbraith (1990), takes place at Harvard University and directly focuses on issues surrounding tenure, curriculum, and school finance issues.

The Role of the Novel

The topic of faculty governance is generally approached through a more traditional, research-oriented perspective. However, novels may provide unique perspectives about academe by illustrating the relationship between academe and the general public, and by contributing a discourse to pursue additional frameworks.

Universities and colleges do not operate independent of the public arena. In fact, we suggest a consistent, complex, and ongoing dynamic between higher education and the general public. The public's conception of academe can affect many aspects of higher education such as funding, the curriculum, donations and gifts, and so forth. Because of this, it is necessary to consider how the public arrives at its conceptions. Few of the general public are privy to the internal workings of a college or university, yet many have an interest in higher education.

How does the general public arrive at an image of higher education? One way is through reading novels. Fiction often reaches a much larger population than publications in scholarly and academic journals. Works of fiction may play a large role in people's conceptions of colleges and universities. For example, most college professors are not befuddled curmudgeons, yet this image is often portrayed in the novel. These inconsistencies between the portrayal of academe in fiction and the actual people and operations of higher education raise a few questions. Foremost among these is how accurate is a novel's portrayal of reality? For example, is the image of the wild, eccentric English professor "true," or is it a combination of reality and fiction? If novels provide even a partial view of reality, what images do they convey about academe?

The Dialectic

The purpose of this paper is to use the dialectic, or exchange of information, to establish a framework, or rationale, for the use of novels in uncovering or more fully portraying the role of governance in higher education. Dialectic refers to the existence of some kind of conversation, or mutually dependent exchange of information. One definition of dialectic is a "tension between conflicting ideas, elements, or ideas" (Encarta World Online Dictionary, 2002). This implies a tension between the novel's depiction of higher education, the conceptions academe has of itself, and the public's image of higher education. An extension of the definition is "the investigation of the truth through discussion, or the art of investigating truth through discussion" (Encarta World Online Dictionary, 2002). This latter definition, in turn, makes an assumption that the true portrayal of academe lies in the interrelatedness of these frames, made possible only by an interplay of sorts. The exploration of the idea of a dialogue between novels and academe is one that is both sensible and revealing. The issue of governance is an important issue, and it is worth considering the many ways in which this can be explored. Essentially, the use of novels in this manner is the creation of a new lens by which to conduct a complex analysis.

Conceptual Framework

The conceptual framework that we used in our analysis of the college novel was the paradigm of organizations as psychic prisons (Morgan, 1997). According to Morgan "organizations are ultimately created and sustained by conscious and unconscious processes—people can become imprisoned in or confined by the images, ideas, thoughts, and actions to which these processes give rise" (p. 215). Psychoanalytic theory provides the theoretical foundation for the psychic prison paradigm. Briefly, organizations are a metaphor, or manifestation of a living organism, with the same conscious and unconscious processes, images, and dysfunctions of a person. As such, they project their unconscious fears, hopes, and anxieties onto their members who then internalize and identify with the images the organization has created of itself. It is, essentially, a symbiotic relationship between the organization and its members. Therefore, people within organizations are trapped not only by their individual psychic prisons, but also by the prison of the collective psyche created by the organization.

The remainder of this paper is divided into three sections. In the first section, three major themes in college novels related to decision making and governance will be described. These three themes are: (1) the curriculum; (2) academic freedom; and (3) tenure. The second section contains an examination of these three themes using the conceptual framework of organizations as psychic prisons. The final section contains our conclusions.

COLLEGE NOVELS AND GOVERNANCE THEME

The Curriculum

One of the most visible aspects of a college or university is its curriculum. Conflicts that focus on curricula often mask internal conflicts between individual faculty members, groups of faculty, and academic disciplines and departments. The curriculum becomes the "terrain" on which personal, intrapersonal, and interpersonal battles are fought and, as such, is a "gold mine" for novelists. Indeed, it takes little imagination to create dysfunctional departments, eccentric professors, troubled students, or misguided research endeavors. After reading colleges novels, one is left with an overall image of the curriculum as a tool to achieve various organizational and personal goals, none of which relate to the education of students.

One way in which the curriculum is a tool is to enhance the status or prestige of an institution. Many of the decisions made regarding curriculum are symbolic and attend only to the image of the school, the department, or individual. In *Foolscap*, by Michael Malone (1991), there is a brief and dismal description of one way in which a curriculum (in this case a history program) is enhanced:

> Six short years ago, a Georgia insecticide king, Class of '56, dying of emphysema, had donated thirty-five million dollars in order to bring renowned historians to Cavendish University so that they might, in the words of the bequest, "teach the great lessons of America's past to the leaders of the world's future." By lavish offers of fat salary, little or no teaching, luxurious subsidized travel junkets, and office suites designed by I.M. Pei, the lucky History Department had promptly hired a handful of celebrity scholars from around the Ivies. As a result, they were soon ranked in the top ten nationwide in three separate polls prominently framed in their gleaming new lobby. (p. 13)

The concern expressed in this excerpt is one of enhancing the status and prestige of the department, and by extension the university. Faculty at the fictitious Cavendish University are hired on the basis of Ivy League reputation; and not on the basis of what they may contribute to the educational purposes of students. Further, the administrators in this novel congratulate themselves on paying lavish salaries to professors who may never even teach. By extension this reveals another concern—the "rankings" that are subsequently used to justify such a maneuver. The legitimacy of these rankings is a concern only for an image of prosperity and further distances curriculum from student concerns.

In other instances curriculum is portrayed as a tool to alleviate boredom. In *A Tenured Professor*, by Kenneth Galbraith (1990), the dean and president of Harvard University are discreetly discussing the mundane routine of "what to teach:"

> "We haven't much business again this week," said the Dean after they exchanged greetings. "It's getting a bit troublesome. I wonder if we

shouldn't propose another change in the curriculum. That's always good for a year or two. Maybe something like an inner core requirement." (p. 114)

The dean seems disappointed at an apparent absence of conflict within the university, almost as if that is something required in order to be reputable. The candid manner in which the dean suggests a random solution is interesting and disturbing. In this case, the curriculum is only a tool in the sense that it provides an outlet, or distraction, from other potential problems including boredom.

Although universities generally attempt to convey the importance of a liberal education, the reality is often quite different. In *Lucky Jim*, by Kingsley Amis (1953), a jaded faculty member has a much more "practical" view of the situation:

> "Well, you know, Jim. You can see the authorities' point of view in a way. We pay for John Smith to enter College here and now you tell us, after seven years, that he'll never get a degree. You're wasting our money. If we institute an entrance exam to keep out the ones who can't read or write, the entry goes down by half, and half of us lose our jobs. And then the other demand: All right, we'll lower the pass mark to twenty percent and give you the quantity that you want, but for God's sake don't start complaining in two years' time that your schools are full of teachers who couldn't pass the General Certificate themselves, let alone teach anyone else to pass it. It's a wonderful position, isn't it?" (p. 174)

In both *Lucky Jim* and *A Tenured Professor* there is an obvious demarcation between integrity and practicality, in addition to an equally disturbing division between faculty and students. The goals of the curriculum, though perhaps stated in terms of student success and well-being, are more often convoluted streams of financial difficulty, personal ambition, and professional incompetence.

In other examples this demarcation is even more pronounced. In *Moo*, by Jane Smiley (1995), the author describes the professional relationships responsible for curricula as laughably woeful:

> It was well-known among the faculty that the governor and the state legislature had lost interest in education some twenty years before and it was only a matter of time before all classes would be taught as lectures, all exams given as computer-graded multiple choice, all subscriptions to professional journals at the library stopped, and all research time given up to committee work and administrative red tape. All the best faculty were known to be looking for other jobs, and this was known to be a matter of indifference to the state board of governors. (p. 19)

The ways in which personal issues become manifest in the curriculum is a common and recurring theme. In fact, many decisions by faculty are entirely the result of personal issues with the curriculum providing the arena by which this can be played out. For example, in *The Handmaid of Desire*, by John L'Heureux (1996), the identity of the English department is at stake, solely because of one diabolically ambitious faculty member, Zachary Kurtz. In the case of academe, as portrayed in the novel, it would appear that lower stakes mean larger politics. In other words, the less there is that *needs* to be addressed, the greater the likelihood of personal politics and more conflict. Consider the following passage, in which Kurtz begins to unveil his plans for the new department:

> At the beginning of the spring quarter, as soon as Robbie was installed as chairman, they would hold another faculty meeting and would vote to dissolve the English department. That is, they would vote to create a new department—he made capital letters in the air—The Department of Theory and Discourse. (pp. 42-43)

He would found this department, he said, and he would run it. At first with Robbie Richter as figurehead chair, and then with a complete takeover, once the *fools'* (those faculty who are not involved in the plotting) voting capacities had been dimmed by retirement or by his actively driving them out.

The English Department, of course, will not actually undergo any real change; instead, this move to a "new" department is only to fulfill the erratic and selfish desires of an individual. A similar situation occurs in *Honest Doubt*, by Amanda Cross (2000). In this novel, a murder mystery, the author consistently criticizes the petty and irrational egos of the faculty:

> Haycock was really serious about reorganizing the department. He had a few colleagues who would go along with him, but on the whole his plan would have been disruptive, to say the least. When he died, I had been planning to put the matter before the president and then take some action. Exactly what action, I can't say; in fact, I don't know. And that's all I can tell you about it. I'm sure the situation would have been resolved without too much fuss. Professors often begin by suggesting extreme measures; that gives them maneuvering room." (p. 185)

Obviously the dysfunction here is quite profound, and the political nature of curriculum disputes is quite obvious. In most cases, the curriculum itself is of little importance, and is merely representative of an ulterior agenda. In any case, curriculum issues are never as simple as they seem, and the politics underlying these disputes are connected to other issues involving governance. Academic freedom is often contested in higher education, and also reveals these same political and personal issues.

Academic Freedom

Academic freedom is premised on the notion that the university is a community of scholars engaged in the pursuit of knowledge, both individually and collective, and both within and outside the classroom. Further, it is considered an invaluable social service rendered by the university to promote and protect the advancement of knowledge; this service can only be performed in an atmosphere free of administrative, political, and religious constraints on thought and expression. While the First Amendment of the Constitution protects any individual's right to freedom of speech and expression, academic freedom extends this basic right to encompass an academic's responsibility to generate and disseminate knowledge in a context free of repression. A second major purpose of academic freedom is to protect faculty's participation in the governance of an institution.

In many of the novels studied for this paper the suppression of academic freedom is quite overt, often to the point of losing any credibility. In *The Male Animal*, by James Thurber (1939), a professor is being pressured into not reading a controversial paper from a long deceased (and misunderstood) political activist:

> ED: Turner, you better think twice before you read anything. I can promise you the trustees will clamp down on any professor who tries anything funny. I'm telling you that for your own good. (p. 44)

Professor Turner, the "male animal," refuses to give in, and eventually this dissension becomes more widely known across campus. His intention to read the paper is published by a rebellious student in the local paper; Turner is advised to deny all charges and *not* read the paper. The governing board, by way of its many lackeys, turns up the pressure, but Turner still refuses:

> ED: I thought Turner was going to deny this story. Papers keep calling *me*—they say he hasn't. Here I am, bearing the brunt of this damn disgraceful attack. "Fascists!" You oughtta heard Si McMillan! And do you know Kressinger's in town from Detroit?
>
> ELLEN: Is he a trustee, too?

DAMON: Oh, yes. Michael certainly exploded this dynamite at a moment when the concentration of trustees is at its thickest.

ED: There goes the new stadium! There goes your Endowment Fund! Unless something is done, and done quick! (p. 63)

Although Thurber makes an impassioned commentary on the importance of academic freedom, his message is ultimately quite simplistic and difficult to take too seriously. Both the dispute and its resolution are predictable and do not provide the moral "gray area" that would likely accompany cases in which academic freedom is a real issue:

TOMMY: He was accused of murder, but thousands of people believe he was executed simply because of the ideas he believed in.

ED: That's a dangerous thing to bring up.

TOMMY: No, it's a dangerous thing to keep down. I'm fighting for a teacher's rights. But if you want to make it political, all right! You can't suppress ideas because you don't like them—not in this country—not yet. This is a university! It's our business to bring what light we can into this muddled world—to try to follow truth! This isn't about Vanzetti. This is about us! If I can't read this letter today, tomorrow none of us will be able to teach anything except what Mr. Keller here and the Legislature permit us to teach. Can't you see what that leads to—what it has led to in other places? We're holding the last fortress of free thought, and if we surrender to prejudice and dictation, we're cowards." (p. 130)

Waller's (1993) *Slow Waltz in Cedar Bend* provides a similar, overly simplistic view of curriculum in terms of academic freedom. Michael Tillman the "maverick" economics professor rebels in an insidious passive-aggressive manner at the standardization of teaching:

But in some way he had never been able to define, graduate school and his early years as a professor had taken the dreams away from him. Something to do with the emphasis on method, with plodding data collection and analysis. Something to do with social scientists trying to operate like physicists, as if the roiling complexities of social reality could be handled in the same way as the study of nature. And something to do with students who cared only for job preparation, who demanded what they called "relevance," and had no real interest in the abstractions he found so lovely, so muchlike a clear, cold mountain stream running through his brain. "Good theory is the most practical thing you can study," he told them. They didn't believe him.

He gave a little speech at a College of Business and Economics faculty meeting. "We are interested, it seems, not in creating, but only in maintaining—maintaining our comfortable, enviable lifestyle. If the taxpayers ever discover what's really going on around here, they'll march on us. We're like the goddamned students and the students are like us dumb bastards: it's come down to cooperate and graduate."

Two heads out of 137 nodded in agreement, 135 wished the dean would get on with the meeting and talk about next year's salary prospects. Michael didn't make anymore speeches after that." (p. 22)

Although Waller's intentions are uncertain, he accomplishes little more than fueling a controversy while providing no solutions or alternatives. Indeed, it seems that Professor Tillman wants to be angry instead of finding ways to improve a system he despises even though it affords him a good living.

The Groves of Academe, by Mary McCarthy (1951), offers a more subtle glimpse of the complexities of academic disputes. The protagonist, Dr. Henry Mulcahy, learns that his contract will not be renewed (he does not yet have tenure). Upon learning this, Mulcahy embarks on a plan that will save his job, in addition to allowing him to play out personal politics. Mulcahy's plan is interesting; he falsely claims that he was once a member of the Communist Party. By doing so, it can only appear that he has been fired for his political beliefs. Mulcahy believes his plan will work because of the nature of his institution:

It [the school] had been founded in the late Thirties by an experimental educator and lecturer, backed by a group of society-women in Cleveland, Pittsburgh, and Cincinnati who wished to strike a middle course between the existing extremes, between Aquinas and Dewey ... they were simply to be free, spontaneous and coeducational. (pp. 61-62)

Mulcahy's plan involves placing all blame and responsibility onto the President, Dr. Hoar. Dr. Hoar had, in fact, made it quite clear to Mulcahy that his position at the school was only temporary; however, once Mulcahy makes a political statement, Hoar is helpless—every claim he makes is now tainted by Mulcahy's accusation. Ultimately, Muclahy is successful and granted a renewal of his contract. What is interesting is the reversal of roles in this novel; Mulcahy is seen as a hero, in some respects, for standing up to the establishment. However, it is also quite clear that he is *wrong*. McCarthy's message, it seems, is that the corruption of the establishment is what created this opportunity for Mulcahy. In either case, it is difficult to identify heroism, and equally difficult to assign blame.

The perceptions of students is also indicative of the role that academic freedom has within a university. *Moo*, by Jane Smiley (1995), demonstrates the timeless battle to expect both enlightenment and obedience from students. In this novel, the majority of the students are from the Midwest and have "enjoyed" a minimum of intellectual challenge. Marly, a student, expresses alarm at a professor's request to engage in "critical thinking":

Marly expressed discomfort with the idea of "critical thinking," the teacher had written the phrase "Critical thinking is to a liberal education as faith is to religion." After the semester, Marly understood that the converse was true also—faith is to a liberal education as critical thinking is to religion, irrelevant and even damaging. (p. 24)

However, this emphasis on critical thinking is not universally endorsed at the university, at least not with the administration. "Chairman X," from the horticulture department is also the campus radical who consistently opposes large corporate interests that threaten the environment. Of course, Chairman X has tenure and is more or less immune to direct threats; instead, the administration tries to wear him down and subdue his radical leanings:

Every day, Chairman X had to endure the pleasant, reasonable voice of Dean Harstad calming him down. "Say," he would remark, "you've been spreading those radical ideas again. The books are there. The short answer-line people just have to re-e-e-ad from the book. Don't make it harder than it is. These folks who call in, they don't like to go off on a tangent, you know. No time for that."

There is clear discrepancy between academic freedom and radicalism. Academic freedom is always protected, and even held in high regard, so long as it does not pose any real danger to the administration. Real dangers include administrative disputes with governing boards or donors, or conflicts that threaten the image or reputation of the institution. In these cases, academic freedom becomes dangerous and, therefore, viewed in negative terms—as an obstruction that the administration must overcome. This reveals the degree to which faculty and administrators will fight to defend an image. Administrators or faculty who suborn or attempt to eliminate academic freedom are portrayed as operating from a position of fear and vulnerability.

Tenure

Tenure is the mechanism by which academic freedom is protected. Yet, in the college novel, it is portrayed as a coveted prize guaranteeing lifetime employment for power hungry, slightly dissolute, and often crazed professoriate. Tenure is fundamentally valuable to the academy and is considered a reasonable response to the highly specialized nature of academic work and the long training period. Van Alstyne (1971) explains and defends tenure with the following statement:

Tenure, accurately and unequivocally defined, lays no claim whatsoever to a guarantee of lifetime employment. Rather, tenure provides only that no person, continuously retained as a full-time faculty member beyond a specified lengthy period of probationary service may thereafter be dismissed without adequate cause. Moreover, the particular standards of "adequate cause" to which the tenured faculty is accountable are themselves wholly within the prerogative of each university to determined through its own published rules, save only those rules may not be applied in a manner that violates the academic freedom or the ordinary personal civil liberties of the individual. In a practical sense, tenure is translatable principally as a statement of formal assurance that hereafter the individuals' professional security and academic freedom will not be placed in question without full academic due process. (p. 328)

However, in the college novels examined for this chapter, tenure was never portrayed in this manner, but instead in other, dysfunctional ways. Tenure is depicted as the big prize and, indeed, a guarantee of life employment. This notion is exemplified in *Foolscap*, when a colleague says to Theo (the main character): "You got tenure! Know what they used to give you with tenure here? Your own personal plot in the Cavendish cemetery! I'm not kidding, tenure *is* forever" (p. 12).

Tenure is also described as a weapon for power struggles and personal vengeance. In *The Handmaid of Desire* (L' Heureux, 1996), Zachary (a faculty member in the English department) is feverishly attempting to become department chair and reform the department to his image. One of his strategies is to ensure that only select faculty are kept in the department. Two untenured colleagues are up for tenure and Zachary plots with two like-minded colleagues on how to get rid of one of them, Francis Xavier Tortorisi:

"And Francis Xavier Tortorisi, it goes without saying, has to *go* without saying ... if you'll forgive the *mot*. He writes those shitty novels for Christ's sake. We shoot him down at tenure." And then to Zachary he said, "What do you have against him, Zack? Aside from the fact that he's a terrible writer and a terrible teacher and a general blight on the aesthetic landscape, what exactly makes you want to exterminate him?"

"He's *fat*. He's a fat fuck and it makes me sick just to look at him"

"So we'll deny him tenure," Robbie Richter said. "Agreed? Which means, in effect, that we'll have to call in favors. We should insist on negative votes, or, where we can't get a negative, at least get an absenteeism. I'll contact my people—all the untenured hires—and Gil, you can work the fools [referring to the rest of the tenured faculty in the department], because they know and like you, sort of, and Zack, well, you have to work from the students on up, I guess." (p. 23)

Rather than being a mechanism for the protection of academic freedom, tenure is characterized as the mechanism to restrict radicalism and promote conformity. In *Moo* (Smiley, 1995), Professor Gift is "fuming" over what he perceives as a lack of loyalty by those in his department who support the promotion to full professor of a colleague (Carolyn Cates) he considers unsuitable. Although there is not a question of tenure in this situation, Gift reflects on the attitudes of his colleagues who support Cates:

> And Helen! Many years ago, he had served on the committee that granted Helen tenure and he had judged her an intelligent and personable young woman, pretty but not too pretty. French but not too French, Italian but not too Italian. Why had she turned on him? (p. 246)

In *A Tenured Professor* (Galbraith, 1990), McCrimmon, a tenured and senior faculty member asks Marvin, then a graduate student at Harvard, about his life plans. Marvin responds "I'm going to be an economist, but I want to make my small contribution to the liberal agenda" (pp. 38-39). McCrimmon responds:

> most unwise. And certainly impractical. You simply won't get tenure. Tenure was originally invented to protect radical professors, those who challenged the accepted order. But we don't have such people anymore at the universities, and the reason *is* tenure. When the time comes to grant it nowadays, the radicals get screened out. That's its principal function. It's a very good system, really—keeps academic life at a decent level of tranquility. (pp. 38-39).

Those who have tenure fear losing the power that it engenders to them. Those who do not have tenure fear never seeing its face. Tenure allows the recipients to retreat into mediocrity. The manor is the last stronghold of the privileged. However, they are losing ground and cling tightly and viciously to their remaining power.

DISCUSSION

Morgan (1997) suggested that organizations are fundamentally governed by "conscious and unconscious processes, with the notion that people can actually be imprisoned in or confined by the images, ideas, thoughts, and actions to which these processes give rise" (p. 215). As a result, organizations begin to take on a life of their own and exert some measure of control over their members. In this paradigm an organization does not necessarily exist to accomplish a tangible, worthwhile task as much as it exists to establish personal and interpersonal meaning. An organization exists to give shape and substance to human existence. Because of this, organizations can often display many of the same dysfunctions that occur within human beings. There are two levels within which this may be observed—within individuals and within groups.

In this discussion, we will examine how the concept of the psychic prison provides a framework by which to analyze the decision-making processes within higher education. In addition, we will discuss fundamental ways in which psychic prisons gain power within organizations in general, and specifically within academic organizations. To accomplish this, three main themes of organizations as psychic prisons and their relationship to faculty governance will be explored. These themes are (1) psychic prisons and sexuality, (2) psychic prisons as defense mechanisms, and (3) psychic prisons and egocentrism

Psychic Prisons and Sexuality

Morgan (1997) explored the ways in which issues surrounding sexuality can surface within an organization and influence the ways in which decisions are made. Two aspects or repressed sexuality within organizations will be discussed; bureaucracy and repressed sexuality, and patriarchal dominance.

Morgan referred to Michel Foucault in making an argument for the powerful effects that result from a need to control and impose order. According to Morgan, "this conflict between organization and sexuality should come as no surprise, for mastery and control of the body is fundamental for control over social and political life. He [Foucault] thus encourages us to note the parallels between the rise of formal organization and the routinization of the human body" (p. 225).

In the novels examined for this paper, the politics within academe are complex and nasty. Indeed, many of the political machinations seem counterintuitive—the lower the stakes, the worse the politics. Higher education, like many organizations, exists as a large and powerful bureaucracy. As such, it exerts a great deal of formal and informal control over its members, repressing individual needs and interests. Power is often unevenly or unclearly dispersed, and the issues in contention (e.g., curricula) are often ambiguous and inane. However, faculty actually have a great deal of power within the bureaucracy, especially those faculty with tenure. This combination of power and repression gives rise to many issues that are fundamentally sexual in nature. In fact, it is rare to encounter a novel that does not have an issue involving some kind of sexual liaison, whether it is among faculty, students, or both.

The Handmaid of Desire (L' Heureux, 1996) provides a good example of the use of sexual manipulation as a tool to impose one's will; in fact, much of the politicking in this novel is accomplished through sexual manipulation. Zachary Kurtz (a contentious, highly political faculty member) at one point describes his countless escapades with students almost as an afterthought. He also hints to an untenured faculty member that it might be in her best interest to accommodate his sexual urges. Kurtz desires to create a new department where he controls the rest of the faculty. His political maneuvering is nothing more than a manifestation of sexual repression. Because he feels trapped or inadequate, Kurtz constantly seeks power and prestige.

Indeed, evidence of this issue is ubiquitous. The existence of a large bureaucracy, coupled with unusual amounts of faculty autonomy, seems to encourage this behavior. Because of this, the sexual repression that inevitably occurs within the organization can more easily find an outlet. The emergence of a need for power and control that results from repressed sexuality is responsible for the aggressive and damaging political maneuvers. This includes abuses involving tenure, the renaming of departments, and the creation of extraneous events. All these manipulations are self-gratifying and also provide evidence of patriarchal dominance. From a psychoanalytic framework this is a major organizational and individual manifestation of repressed sexuality.

The existence of a patriarchal framework dominating organizations is nothing new. Generally, organizations support masculine values such as aggression and competition, and rewards members who display these traits. An analysis of these novels basically supports this assumption. Although there is an obvious attempt to place power in the hands of women and minorities, most positions of real power (formal or otherwise) are still relegated to white males.

This is more obvious in some novels than in others. *The Male Animal* (Thurber, 1939), for example, is interesting in this regard. In this short play, the "male animal" is an English professor who refuses to back down to administrators who threaten him with dismissal if he reads a controversial paper. The major conflict in the play is between the professor and a male rival who is a former football star at the college. The professor, by refusing to back down on an issue of academic freedom, is portrayed as even more masculine than the stereotypically accepted version masculinity—a football star. The images and results of repressed sexuality in the college novel reveal the existence of patriarchal framework underlying college governance that can still not be understated.

Dependency and Defense Mechanisms

When using the metaphor of the psychic prison, it is important to understand the role that personal issues and desires play in regard to decision making. Many of the decisions made by faculty and administrators in college novels have very little do with practicality or fairness. In fact these issues can often be secondary to other impulses. In addition to the powerful role that sexuality has on the unconscious, many decisions involve the interplay of defense mechanisms and dependency issues within the psyche. The involvement of either (or both) of these factors can greatly influence the decision-making process.

Morgan (1997) suggested that "it is possible to understand the structure, processes, culture, and even the environment of an organization in terms of the unconscious defense mechanisms developed by its members to cope with individual and collective anxiety" (p. 231). Organizations are generally designed to accomplish a task of some kind; however, when this "task focus" becomes foggy, tensions inevitably arise within the organization. This in turn promotes disorder among members of the organization causing these individuals to establish a defensive posture towards the organization (Morgan, 1997, pp. 231-232).

In *Moo* the politics of the university are stated in no uncertain terms:

It was well known among the legislators that the faculty as a whole was determined to undermine the moral and commercial well-being of the state, and that supporting a large and nationally famous university with state monies was exactly analogous to raising a nest of vipers in your own bed (Smiley, 1995, p. 19).

The characters and plot of *Moo* strongly support this statement. Most of the faculty and all of the administrators *react* to situations, and generally do behave like a "nest of vipers." For example, the Provost, Ivar Harstad, lives in perpetual fear of his secretary, Mrs. Walker (he never drops the formal title) and suffers from a conflicting desire to simultaneously destroy her and still win her approval. Mrs. Walker is politically connected across the campus and is feared by both faculty and administration alike. The Dean, Ivar's brother Nils, suffers from this same malady, and the result is both comical and pathetic. However, it is also important to note that in being humbled by their secretary, both Ivar and Nils internalize a great deal of anger and resentment. These feelings manifest in abuses of power on other faculty.

This anger is directed especially at Chairman X, the head of the horticulture department. Harstad hates Chairman X for his "radical" ideas about the environment and myriad social issues and, in turn, Chairman X has a hated adversary of his own, Dr. Lionel Gift. Dr. Gift is a professor of economics and the highest paid faculty member on campus, a distinction earned through shady and dubious means. His latest endeavor is helping to arrange the financing for a gold mine in Costa Rica that will destroy large amounts of natural rain forest. Chairman X learns of this and vows to do everything he can to stop Gift.

What is interesting about this particular scenario is Gift's motivations for doing this in the first place. Although he is motivated to a large degree by money, the money is only a means to an end. What Gift really wants is respect and notoriety, and he focuses all his energy on achieving these things. As a result, Gift is constantly in conflict and uses both his formal and informal power to defend against either real or perceived threats to his ego. To achieve this, Gift relies on defense strategies that are primarily symbolic:

> One profitable practice, in Dr. Gift's view, was meeting with the committee once or twice before any departmental materials were referred to it, and so he sent out a memo calling a meeting in the second week of classes, and so he reserved the economics seminar room, and so he sat at the head of the walnut seminar table and watched the other members file in. (Smiley, 1995, p. 33)

Throughout the book it is quite evident that Dr. Gift will go to great lengths to maintain an image of power, prestige, and invulnerability. Unfortunately, Gift's psychological dysfunction results in poor teaching, damaged faculty relations, and ecological mayhem. Often money is seen as the prime motivator in situations like these; however, an analysis of Dr. Gift's intentions reveals the limitations of this logic. Money operates here as a symbol on two levels. It operates most obviously as a metaphor for prestige, power, and positional strength. However, it also symbolic of the ways in which Gift's psychology is a major factor in decision making.

Egocentrism and Narcissism

According to Morgan (1997), most organizations fundamentally operate on a single underlying principle—to reproduce themselves at any cost. When viewed in this light, the motives of individual members within an organization tend to make more sense. According to this principle, members of an organization act consciously or unconsciously in order to protect the organization. Unfortunately, what people perceive to be helpful, and what actually *is* helpful can be quite different.

Morgan suggested a theory called autopoiesis, the ability of organizations to renew or replicate themselves (p. 253). Many organizations become quite adept at this self-replication. However, replication is not always in the best interests of an organization and can even lead to its eventual demise. In other words, mindless replication can be a very dangerous thing. Morgan describes two types of organizations that tend to display self-destructive behaviors—egocentric organizations and narcissistic organizations.

Morgan described narcissistic organizations as "interacting with projections of themselves" and suggests that many of the problems with this type of organizations are simply a matter of creating and maintaining a particular image (p. 256). Narcissistic organizations are in love with a created, idealized image of themselves. However, like narcissism in individuals, this is an extremely destructive and unfulfilling state of mind.

In *Ravelstein*, by Saul Bellow (2000), we are introduced to the famous professor whose name graces the title, Abe Ravelstein. Professor Ravelstein is an influential professor of political science whose students have gone on to positions of power and prestige in the government. However, Ravelstein also has a reputation as a difficult and arrogant man. Interestingly, Professor Ravelstein, in the twilight of his career, publishes a book that goes on to become an international best seller, making him rich and famous.

Even prior to this publication Ravelstein focused the majority of his energy on an image of himself that he felt satisfied both the academic and popular communities. His persona as the "brilliant but anguished professor" becomes a trap—it simply is not possible to satisfy those kinds of ambitions. Even when he publishes his book, Ravelstein is still trapped by a vision of himself. He is able to convince himself, most of the time, that his real life and this image are synonymous. However, like any narcissistic entrapment he finds himself lost in a reflection and missing out on the reality of his existence.

A similar commentary about the dangers of narcissistic entrapment is contained within *The Groves of Academe*, by Mary McCarthy (1951). In this novel, set in a small liberal arts school, an untenured professor loses his position in the English department. The motives behind this event are unclear. In any case, Henry Mulcahy, the professor, develops a cunning plan—he spreads rumors that he was a member of the Communist Party. The administration, he claims, discovered this and fired him. Mulcahy's scheme is actually quite ingenious because the school revels in its status as a "liberal" college, one in which free speech would never be infringed:

> It [the school] had been founded in the late Thirties by an experimental educator and lecturer, backed by a group of society-women in Cleveland, Pittsburgh, and Cincinatti who wished to strike a middle course between the existing extremes, between Acquinas and Dewey . . . they were simply to be free, spontaneous, and coeducational. What the founder had in mind was a utopia. (pp. 61-62)

It is obvious that the school loves this vision of itself; however, the school is not as liberal as it pretends. The important distinction is that it is forced to maintain this image, regardless of whether or not it is actually true. Mulchay's scheme is successful because he understands the school's inability to escape its image. The organization loves itself when it is liberal, free, and spontaneous. It does not matter if this is really true, as long as this image is maintained. As a result, Mulcahy is reinstated and the school goes about its normal business; the psychic entrapment here is both pronounced and profound.

Morgan (1997) explained that egocentric organizations are "those [organizations] that have a fixed notion of who they are and sustain that identity at any cost. In enacting and dealing with their environment in an egocentric way, organizations often do not understand their own complexity and the numerous recursive loops on which they depend" (p. 259). The egocentric organization is quite similar in many ways to the narcissistic organization—both are trapped by a vision of themselves. However, egocentric organizations are trapped by arrogance and not by self-love.

Every novel that we studied evidenced elements of egocentrism. From this it seems easy to suggest that at least the fictional image of faculty decision making and governance in academe is based on egocentric motives. The academic organization cannot afford, for its own sake, to believe there are limits to its power and control. For example, in *A Tenured Professor*, the faculty relied heavily on the fact that they were indeed Harvard professors. Certainly, it seems incongruent to think of Harvard without thinking about the pivotal role they (and other Ivy League schools) play in our conceptions of higher education. For good or bad, they are seen as possessing a certain arrogance, and these novels do little to dispel this thinking.

There are numerous examples that show the egocentric decisions made by faculty and administrators. Curriculum and instruction, presumably a primary focus at any school, are routinely ignored and downplayed. Those professors who attempt to do well by their students generally find themselves in trouble. Professor Cady, for example, in *Novemberfest* (Weesner, 1994), failed to achieve tenure, partly because he focused too much on his teaching. This sentiment is echoed in *Slow Waltz in Cedar Bend* (Waller, 1993); Professor Tillman has frequent conflicts with the administration, often regarding the role professors have in terms of teaching.

Why is egocentrism so apparently so universal in the college novel? A complex interaction of factors might account for this. Clearly, colleges and universities have existed for a long time, and they will certainly exist indefinitely. Given this, it is safe to assume that institutions of higher education, as organizations, have learned to replicate those factors that are most suited to survival. Research universities, using this framework, are probably wise to focus more on grants and research than on student concerns. Historically, this has been effective, and the nature of this theory assumes replication of successful models.

If this is even partially true, than universities are not solely to blame for lackluster or inferior curricula, or for failing to properly educate students. Instead, this "blame" falls on the interaction between society and academe. If poor instruction truly had an adverse affect on schools, than the organizations would adapt to ensure survival. If dysfunctional faculty truly damaged the workings of the school, than there might be fewer instances of such behavior. In any case, the egocentrism is portrayed in novels and quite real and common.

CONCLUSION

The psychic prison is manifest in three ways: (1) The emergence of sexual issues; (2) The overreliance on defense mechanisms; and (3) The tendency to display egocentrism and/or narcissism. In each case, the unconscious plays a powerful role in shaping the nature of the organization, and strongly influences the ways in which decisions are made. To further complicate matters, these factors do not work in isolation—instead, they may act alone or in interaction with other. Also, these factors are certainly influenced by external factors.

What is perhaps most disturbing about the portrayal of faculty's role in decision making and governance in the college novel is the manner in which faculty are depicted. Generally, they are mean-spirited, selfish, and narrow-minded individuals whose major concerns are immediate satisfaction and self-interest; these interests focus on control, power, and dominance. Morgan's (1997) paradigm of organizations as psychic prisons seems to provide an accurate framework to organize characterizations of faculty as represented in college novels. Indeed, their behaviors and attitudes reflect a symbiotic relationship with academe.

Institutions of higher education obviously manipulate and control public opinion, however, these same institutions are also greatly impacted by the public's perception. This article suggests that the public arrives at this perception in myriad ways. The depiction of higher education in fiction (and novels in particular) is a valuable lens by which to elucidate this complex interaction. Novels strongly impact public perception, both creating and sustaining organizational images of higher education. Whether these images are *accurate* is not really the issue; instead, it is important to consider what people *believe* is true. Decisions are based on perception, and these perceptions may or not be aligned with reality.

This paper uses the *dialectic* as an impetus for discussion and criticism. The interaction, or conversation, between higher education and fiction is an important tool for understanding organizational and decision-making dynamics in higher education. The "truth" of this dynamic cannot exist independent of this interaction. In other words, college novels are not revealing in and of themselves unless they are placed in a framework that allows for and encourages critical reflection.

Generally these institutions are depicted quite unfavorably in novels. These negative depictions are remarkably consistent, suggesting a well-established and stable public perception. In turn, it is logical to suggest that this influences the interaction between higher education and the public, and that this fiction is more "real" than previously suspected and strongly impacts the governance of these organizations.

The psychic prison metaphor is an important consideration. Organizationally, these institutions are quite unique and operate within a complex and dysfunctional paradigm. Faculty often enjoy a great deal of autonomy within the organization, but the pressures of scholarship, teaching, and political maneuvering cannot be overstated. Although there is a formal hierarchy, this structure is often muddled and unworkable; instead faculty are forced to operate within a quagmire of uncertainty and ambiguity. Because of this "small" issues (like the naming of a department) are often of critical importance.

The organization is shaped by this interplay. Faculty create images of themselves within the organization as a coping mechanism, and these images then influence the organization itself. Personal dysfunctions become organizational, and the organization becomes bureaucratic and stifling, further perpetuating the petty and personal politics.

In any case, the picture of higher education within novels is an interesting journey that is both humorous and depressing, and enlightening and confusing. Indeed, higher education is a microcosm of society, but it is one that has evolved on a separate path.

REFERENCES

Amis, K. (1953). *Lucky Jim*. London: Camelot Press.
Bellow, S. (2000). *Ravelstein*. New York: Penguin Putnam.
Cross, A. (2000). *Honest doubt*. New York: Ballantine.
Encarta World Online Dictionary. (2002). Retrieved March, 2002, from http://dictionary.msn.com/
Fitzgerald, F. S. (1920). *This side of paradise*. New York: Charles Scribner's Sons.
Galbraith, J. K. (1990). *A tenured professor*. Boston: Houghton Mifflin.
Kundera, M. (1988). *The art of the novel*. New York: Grove Press.
L' Heureux, J. (1996). *The handmaid of desire*. New York: SoHo Press.
Malone, M. (1991). *Foolscap*. New York: Little, Brown, & Company.

McCarthy, M. (1951). *The groves of academe.* New York: Harcourt, Brace and Company.

Morgan, G. (1997). *Images of organization.* Thousand Oaks, CA: Sage.

Smiley, J. (1995). *Moo.* New York: Alfred A. Knopf.

Thurber, J. (1939). *The male animal.* New York: Samuel French.

Van Alstyne, W. (1971). Tenure: A summary, explanation and "defense." *AAUP Bulleting, 57*(3), 328-333.

Waller, R. J. (1993). *Slow waltz in cedar bend.* New York: Warner Books.

Weesner, T. (1994). *Novemberfest.* Hanover, NH: University Press of New England.

CHAPTER 9

FACULTY GOVERNANCE IN COMMUNITY COLLEGES

A Distinct Perspective of Broad-Based Decision Making

Myron L. Pope
University of Oklahoma

Community colleges present a unique and progressive form of American postsecondary education. These institutions provide higher education opportunities to a large portion of the country's minority populations while concurrently serving a large number of adult and part-time students. They utilize a highly trained faculty, which numbers more than 120,000 nationwide (part-time and full-time), who provide a variety of educational services, from vocational to collegiate courses. These colleges are complex in their efforts to meet the demands of local governing boards while also attempting to meet the unique demands of their diverse student population (Katsinas, 1996).

Most community colleges have an open-access admission policy, which means they accept students with a variety of educational preparation levels. This philosophy creates a pool of students who range from levels of literacy comparable to those taking lower-division courses at a selective

Policy and University Faculty Governance, 119–136
Copyright © 2003 by Information Age Publishing

four-year college to students who are marginally literate. This variation was particularly evident as higher education witnessed a decline in college-age students and as there was a decline in the scholastic abilities of secondary education graduates and drop-outs (Cohen & Brawer, 1996). The faculty of these institutions has been instrumental in providing curricular development and implementation to accommodate these issues.

Community college faculty members are a group of highly trained individuals who provide vocational, collegiate, and remedial based instruction (Duke, 1997). Unlike their four-year college counterparts, these individuals' have a primary role focused on instructional activities with occasional service-related duties (Brint & Karabel, 1989). They must be student-centered in their approach to ensure the success of the diverse abilities, interests, and goals of their students. Therefore, it is important that they spend a significant amount of time teaching and working with students (Rifkin, 1997). Community college faculty have been instrumental in assisting these institutions to provide the leadership role in the reconceptualization of how education is offered in the United States.

Consequently in their efforts to provide a high quality level of education and leadership in the provision of higher education opportunities, community college leaders must maintain quality relationships with business, industry, and community groups (Sorrentino & Hines, 1994). Hood (1997) noted that this relationship building should also exist within these institutions, as presidents attempt to establish positive working conditions, specifically with their faculty.

During the past decade, business and industry leaders have worked to enhance profitability through attention to internal operations. This attention, often noted in total quality management and continuous quality improvement programs within the private sector, has subsequently been addressed in higher education. One of these movements has been the focus on "teaming," empowerment, or participative decision making (Kerr, 1991). The results of this desire to focus on broad-based decision making to validate policy making and decision making are faculty senates, councils, and forums composed of faculty and sometimes staff members (Pope & Miller, 2000a). This involvement is not a novelty, as faculty have long participated in the administrative process to some extent. However, the interest in participation waned for various reasons, and now it is experiencing resurgence. Gilmour (1991) reported that 60-75% of all community colleges have some form of faculty governance unit, which means that approximately 700-875 of these units have these bodies.

Faculty governance units have addressed a variety of topics from budget priorities to on-campus smoking policies (Garavalia, Miller, & Miles, 1999). Carlisle and Miller (1999) noted that during a five-year period, faculty governance bodies challenged presidents, authorized strikes related to employee benefits, and expressed concerns regarding institutional direction. These are consistent with the notion that faculty governance units exist to serve in a watchdog role in balancing administrative decisions concerning institutional trends and issues relevant to faculty (Armstrong, Miller, & Newman, 2001).

These findings provide a gateway to further understand the process of faculty involvement in governance in community colleges. As these institutions are distinct in their role in the provision of higher education, they also are unique in their governance processes. Thus, the purpose of this chapter will be to provide a perspective of the role of the participative governance process, to define the structures and processes of shared governance, and to assess the future of faculty governance in America's community colleges. Specifically, the chapter will be guided by the uniqueness of the community college to higher education and how this distinct atmosphere affects administrative decision making.

THE ORGANIZATION OF DECISION MAKING IN COMMUNITY COLLEGES

The typical vision of institutional governance has been achieved through a passing of tradition and expectation in terms of process method and traditionally expected outcome (Kerr, 1991). A chief executive officer or college president, who is responsible for the day-to-day operations of the institution, serves at the liberty of a board of trustees who selects this individual. Even though broad consensus building and recommendations from senior administrators are prominent in the decision-making process, the public generally views the position of the president and the academic and economic image of the institution as being synonymous. The image of the president is one of power and prestige and typically one of the most visible members of the community (Colgan, 2001).

Regardless, faculty historically have been involved in institutional decision making. The American Association of University Professors created the Committee on the Place and Function of Faculty in University Governance and Administration in 1916, specifically acknowledging the role of faculty in governance (Keller, 1983). This body, also recognized as "Committee T" (Schuster, 1991), was developed to create standards for campus governance and grew in response to business and industry pressure to change the curriculum and organization of the academe. Committee T, worked jointly with the Association of Governing Boards to develop the statement in 1966 that focused on the rights and responsibilities of the faculty, president, and trustees.

R. E. Miles (1965) provides a representation of thinking that is a shift from scientific management theory to more of a human relations approach of organizational behavior. In this new environmental mindset, the individual and their needs are valued. At the time of Committee T, this has relevance to the burgeoning Progressive Era that argued that organizations do not "do wrong" although individuals in those organizations might. Therefore, the involvement of the individual in the decision making of the organization is significant in increasing productivity and feelings of concern for the work environment (Sergiovanni & Starratt, 1988).

Typically, faculty involvement in institutional governance takes the form of participation in a faculty senate, forum, or other form of council. This forum allows faculty to participate in decision making and policy formation (Gilmour, 1991). Faculty forums usually confront the biggest conflicts with administrators regarding the allocation of resources, policy formation, and institutional vision. Floyd (1985) noted also that these bodies handle the more individualized aspects of faculty welfare, such as tenure, academic freedom, program termination, resource reallocation, and other such issues. Miller, Garavalia, and McCormack (1997) studied this complex relationship between administrators and faculty and concluded that faculty participation and power were linked. They utilized a modified version of Murphy's (1991) model for parent participation in school management to define this relationship. Their stratified model proposed that manipulation of faculty in decision making was a form of nonparticipation, that tokenism was a therapeutic reason for involvement and placation, and finally that faculty power was exemplified by partnerships with administration, delegated power, or control over decision making (see Figure 9.1). This model asserts that there is a direct positive correlation between increased levels of involvement with greater levels of faculty power (Miller, Garavalia, & McCormack, 1997).

Even though many view faculty participation through the faculty forum conduit, the Carnegie Foundation for the Advancement of Teaching

8	Faculty control	
7	Delegated power	Degrees of faculty power
6	Partnership	
5	Placation	
4	Consultation	Degrees of tokenism
3	Informing	
2	Therapy	Nonparticipation
1	Manipulation	

Figure 9.1.   Ladder of faculty involvement in governance.

(1982) stated that faculty authority comes to focus most directly at the academic department level. At this level, faculty make decisions about what and how courses should be taught, what research should be conducted, how and who should be hired in the department to conduct research and teach, and also what students will receive degrees. Baldridge (1971) stated that power at the institutional level was diffuse because of the differences in values, fields, and structures of individual units. Faculty were more predisposed to focus on the governance of their area unless the issue at the institutional level directly affected their department.

Despite varying perceptions of definitions and levels of involvement in decision making by faculty members, there has been an acceptance by many of these individuals of the process due to the benefits to their welfare and existence. Miller, Vacik, and Benton (1998) reported that faculty members in community colleges in the southeastern United States who had varying levels of involvement in their campuses governance process were convinced that the process was significant in providing a voice for the faculty in decision making. Representative faculty bodies involved in the governance process has also been identified as an "antidote to over-bureaucratization" (Williams, Gore, Broches, & Lostoski, 1987, p. 630). This perception is significant in achieving good decision making in an environment where many administrators are considered to be self-serving (Bergmann, 1991) and are more concerned with their image, reputations, and careers (Mason, 1982). From a more positive perspective, Evans (1999) contended that faculty involvement in the governance process was instrumental in creating a consensus across campus while also providing faculty with a sense of ownership in organizational decision making.

As there are many benefits to the involvement of faculty in the decision making process, many perceive that there are many barriers to the practice also. Pope and Miller (2000b) noted that the practice might promote an atmosphere of resentment because administrators feel that faculty are attempting to do their jobs. They also reported that involvement slowed the decision-making process. There have been several state and federal legal decisions that restrict faculty from participating extensively in the governance process (A. S. Miles, 1987). These decisions, which have limited faculty to classroom instruction, include, *Conner v. Meyer, Minnesota State Board of Postsecondary Education v. Knight,* and *Ballard c. Blunt* (Miles, Miller, & Anderson, 1996).

Another significant factor in the faculty involvement in governance debate revolves around the lack of rewards. As many senior faculty members may have perceptions that faculty senates are manipulated by the administration, they perceive very little need for the existence of and involvement in these bodies (Cybert, 1979). Likewise, junior faculty members may be advised not to participate in the governance process because it will divert them from their teaching responsibilities, the area most recognized in tenure and promotion decisions (Floyd, 1985). Despite the apparent significance of participating in governance, the lack of rewards and the time demands can make the process unappealing. In many cases, this perception leads to an "episodic phenomenon" where faculty enter and leave the decision-making process only when time and interest in the issue are deemed important (Williams et al., 1987).

THE AMERICAN COMMUNITY COLLEGE

For more than 100 years, community colleges have played a significant role in providing opportunity and equity for those interested in enrolling in higher education. From the first college, Joliet in Chicago in 1901, the transfer function has been a significant part of the overall goals of community colleges. However, this mission has expanded over the years to be more inclusive of the interests of the community, business, and industry. Paralleling these efforts has been a commitment to providing access to diverse clientele through an open-door admission policy. Due to this unique philosophy, the role of faculty members on these campuses is quite different than their counterparts at four-year institutions of higher education.

The question of a community college mission is one that is changing frequently. With many states adopting articulation agreements with two-year and four-year colleges, the effort provided to vocational education has decreased. One of the primary local area service provisions community colleges have typically made is local workforce preparation. The desire to function merely as a junior college focused on transfer programming can have substantially negative impacts on rural and nonrural workforce retention, small business development, economic development, and adult literacy programs.

Faculty

The community college professorate has a distinct set of characteristics due to the nature of the institutions' mission, size, diversity, and background. Approximately, 45% of the faculty at these institutions were 49 years of age or older in 1992, while another 37% were between the ages of 40 and 49. Of the faculty members teaching at community colleges, 44% teach part-time (National Center for Education Statistics [NCES], 1997). Many of these individuals have historically had their professional origins in the secondary school sector (Gahn & Twombly, 1998). In 1993, women faculty members represented 44% of the faculty teaching at community colleges (Cohen & Brawer, 1996). As more community colleges are witnessing the enrollment of more minority students, they have attempted to likewise hire more minority faculty. In 1992, minority faculty, which included African American, Asian, Hispanic, and Native American, represented 14.5% of the full-time faculty in community colleges (NCES, 1994).

Community college faculty members focus their efforts primarily on teaching, with high expectations additionally for institutional service. The Commission on the Future of Community Colleges, as part of the American Association of Community and Junior Colleges (1988), defined the goal of these institutions in this way:

> At the center of building community there is teaching. Teaching is the heartbeat of the educational enterprise and, when it is successful, energy is pumped into the community, continuously renewing and revitalizing the institution. Therefore, excellence in teaching is the means by which the vitality of the college is extended and a network of intellectual enrichment and cultural understanding is built. (pp. 7-8)

Consequently, this group of faculty, which is estimated to be 120,000 in number, has high levels of expertise and specialization in their content areas. Student success is placed into the hands of faculty members who are required to combine effective communication and curriculum development skills to serve the needs of nontraditional students who are completing lower-level courses for transfer or programs focusing on vocational or occupational training. Hawthorne (1991) wrote that this generation of community college faculty were the "molders and definers" (p. 365) of the existing community college structure and policy, simply because in many institutions the first generation of faculty are just now retiring and being replaced.

In many community colleges, the faculty are confronted with two distinct challenges: heavy teaching loads and academically under-prepared students. These faculty use instructional and assessment methods that will accommodate the unique needs of the underprepared student (Palmer, 1992). In comparison to their counterparts at four-year institutions who teach only 10 to 14 hours per week, this group spends 15 or more hours per week teaching. In these hours, faculty teach 75 to 150 students. They rely heavily on lecture and lecture-discussion as the primary form of instruction to accommodate this large number of students. Also, they use multiple-choice examinations instead of essays or other complex writing assessments due to the complexity of the underprepared student's literacy levels (Rifkin, 1998). Overall nationally, this group reported that caring for students was the most important aspect of their professional role on their campuses (Rifkin, 1997).

The involvement of faculty in the community college in research has become a topic of substantial debate (Vaughan, 1992; Palmer, 1992; Cohen & Brawer, 1977). Laab (1987) stated that this may be due in part to the proliferation of doctorates among faculty within the community college that desire salary incentives and promotion. Boyer (1990) argued that community college professors should be actively involved in research due to the unique teaching and learning experiences that exist on these campuses. He also suggested that these individuals should be the leaders in contributing to the scholarship related to how students learn, especially those from less advantaged backgrounds. In the report of the Commission on the Future of Community Colleges (1988) the classroom researcher was described as:

> one who is involved in the evaluation of his or her own teaching and learning, even as it takes place. Such a person should be trained to be a careful observer of the teaching process, to collect feedback on what and how well students learn, and to evaluate the effectiveness of instruction. (p. 27)

Further, it has been suggested that participation in research assists faculty in remaining current in their professional areas and consequently improves teaching (Bell, 1992; Vaughan, 1988). These are all contrary to Laab (1987) who argued that the participation of community college faculty in research would undermine teaching quality and the open-admission philosophy.

Research has shown that community college faculty members are relatively content with their profession and their job responsibilities (Rifkin, 1997). These faculty at institutions in the southeastern United States were also satisfied with their level of participation in the governance process. They agreed that their immersion in committee activity, which allowed them to participate in institutional planning, decision making, and resource allocations, was satisfactory to them (Miller, Vacik, & Benton, 1998). Similarly, faculty professed that the psychology of teaching is enhanced when they have an opportunity to participate in the governance process (Miller, Garavalia, & McCormack, 1997).

Community College Faculty Roles and Purposes in Inclusive Decision Making

There is little literature related to the design and types of faculty governance units that exist in community colleges; however, a cursory review of faculty senates on the World Wide Web provides some examples. Though these units were quite distinct in their nature, they were all defined as bodies utilized to provide faculty voice in campus governance.

The most visible title of these bodies seemed to be Faculty or Academic Senates (Salt Lake Community College, Glendale Community College, Broward Community College). These bodies had regularly scheduled, formal meetings where they discussed issues related to academic and other faculty concerns. At some community colleges, the term Faculty Forum was synonymous with the Faculty Senate (Central Oregon Community College, Bergen Community College). Finally, a Faculty Association was also identified as a form of nomenclature for the faculty governance unit (Valencia Community College, Suffolk Community College).

Representation within these bodies differed from campus to campus. In a most cases, a representative form of governance existed. The senate or council consisted of individuals who were elected by their peers to represent their concerns at meetings (Valencia Community College, Suffolk Community College, Glendale Community College, Daytona Community College, Seminole Community College, Tidewater Community College, Broward Community College). On some smaller campuses, the prevalent form of representation seemed to be a town hall focus where any individual faculty member could come and present their concerns. In this latter model, the vote of each individual person present at meetings was counted in elections, as opposed to a representative doing so for their affiliated area (Central Oregon Community College).

There were some campuses that did not have any of these aforementioned entities. However, on many of these campuses, there were comparable bodies identified as staff senates or institutional senates, which were bodies that consisted of some combination of faculty, staff, and students. In almost all cases, representatives from within each of these constituent groups were elected to represent their area within the governance body's meeting (Capital Community College, Massachusetts Community College).

There are many types and designs of faculty governance units within community colleges around the country; however, there is no specific research that addresses this taxonomy. Thus, there is a need for research that will eliminate the ambiguity for individuals analyzing the process. To eliminate some of the perplexity in this text, the term faculty senate will be used to designate those bodies that are responsible for community college faculty governance.

Topics Discussed by Community College Faculty Senates

In general, faculty exercise a good deal of control over decision making regarding the curriculum and other related areas. However, their ability to be involved in broad-based decision making at the institutional level is significant in defining the existence of a faculty senate. At this level of participation, the faculty senate has a role in concerns related to salaries and benefits, budget and institutional policy, and also academic standards. In the latter issue, faculty senate is instrumental in directly making decisions about curriculum reform, raising admission requirements, and implementing graduate requirements. However in issues related to participation in institutional decision making, the faculty senate serves in the capacity of advisor to the president and the board of trustees (Colgan, 2001).

One research effort has been successful in further contributing to the literature base regarding faculty governance, the National Data Base on Faculty Involvement in Governance (NDBFIG). In 1993, the NDBFIG was created to increase the understanding of broad-based decision making on college campuses. The NDBFIG was a five-year research initiative that was affiliated with the University of Alabama. This research has provided a substantial amount of literature to the field, including Kang, Newman, and Miller's (1998) report of the moderate communication and writing apprehension level's of faculty senate presidents, Miller, Garavalia, and McCormack's (1997) findings that involvement in governance activities was positively correlated to teaching effectiveness, Miles, Miller, and Anderson's (1996) research that found that there was no legal basis for faculty involvement in administrative policy or decision making, and several other findings. The latest contribution to this research data was the work focusing on community college cogovernance between faculty and administration (Armstrong, Miller, & Newman, 2001).

In this study, a case analysis of a moderate-sized community college in the southeast was conducted. One of the more significant aspects of this analysis was the collection of data related to the motions considered during an 11-year period. The analysis focused on the faculty senate, as well as the faculty senate council, which was the elected body charged with organizing, directing, and supporting the actions of the larger faculty senate. Through this analysis, topics for motion were quite diverse, including issues related to campus security and safety, campus smoking policy, updating the name of the institution, defining full-time faculty, as well as the ratio of full-time and part-time faculty, and supporting the president's pursuit of equity funding for faculty and staff salaries (Armstrong, Miller, & Newman, 2001).

Characteristics of Community College Faculty Senate Leaders

As faculty senates contribute significantly to the institution in terms of decision making, it is important that these bodies have adequate leadership. This leadership is provided in the form of an elected chair. The chair is important in team building and authority delegation (Phelan,

1996). As a team builder, it is important for the leader to provide the vision, but it is equally important that this individual empower and include all constituencies in the decision-making process (Hilosky & Watwood, 1997). Likewise, this inclusion in the decision-making process is significant in that these individuals willingness to accept the decision outcome (Miller & Seagren, 1993). However, there are other skills and tasks that are important factors in being successful in the chair role.

In a national study of community college faculty governance leaders at 100 community, junior, and technical colleges, Pope and Miller (2000a) analyzed the skills and tasks perceived the most critical in the success of the faculty governance chair. This group of faculty leaders indicated that organizational skills, leadership, and written communication were the most important skills necessary for effective service. This reflected a view that these leaders are important in identifying goals, effectively communicating them to all constituents, and establishing a framework through which these goals may be achieved. In terms of tasks necessary in leading a faculty governance unit, this group perceived that developing personal networks and linkages, developing databases for governance unit decision making, and obtaining and allocating resources were the most important.

In a similar study, Pope and Miller (2000b) analyzed community college faculty governance leaders to determine their most noteworthy stressors and communication apprehension levels. The study found that respondents perceived obtaining program and financial approval and high self-expectations as being the most significant stressors as faculty leaders. Based on this groups rating of their personal oral and written apprehension, it was identified that leaders with higher oral communication apprehension levels "experience higher distress from the activity of completing paperwork on time" (p. 635). Those faculty governance leaders with higher writing apprehension levels were more likely to feel greater stress from preparing manuscripts. These findings were significant in providing a model of the tasks and stressors involved in this critical role, as well as identifying the characteristics that should be considered when selecting a faculty governance leader in the community college.

Determining the Success of Community College Faculty Senates

Some community college faculty are skeptical of the governance process and hesitate in participating. Many of the more senior faculty are reluctant to participate and question the significance of the senate (Cybert, 1979). This is due in part to distrust of administrators and collective disinterest in the process because most of the issues do not directly affect them (Clark, 1970, Floyd, 1985, Williams et al., 1987). Consequently, this decision not to participate leads to a political environment where only a few faculty participate and act merely on personal political agendas. Administrators have little respect for faculty senates in this environment, and thus they acknowledge collaboration just because it is politically correct to do so (Weingartner, 1996). Therefore, the most important question seems to focus on how effective faculty senates are when they operate in these types of settings.

One view of the effectiveness of the faculty senate may lie in its passage of motions. The assumption may be that the greater the consensus of an issue the more relevant it is to significant campus issues. Armstrong et al. (2001) found that 85% of the motions made by the faculty council and senate were passed during their analysis of 11 years of these bodies' deliberations at Jefferson State Community College. Their perception was that despite the variety in the types of topics moved, the two bodies served as focal points for debate and verbalization of concerns on issues that were important to the institution and the faculty as a whole. The high percentage of acceptance of these motions represents their individual levels of significance, and consequently recognizes the senate's effectiveness in the decision-making process.

Weingartner (1996) wrote that the effectiveness of the faculty senate is dependent on two conditions. The first condition focuses on the substance of their discussions, the quality of the coverage regarding these discussions, and finally the quality of the conclusions. The second condition holds that the universal implementation of these deliberations is paramount in defining the effectiveness of faculty senates. However, in order for this process to be fully effective, it must be a collaborative effort with the administration, as opposed to a consultative effort. This latter effort is not considered effective because the decision is not made jointly, but merely consultation with the faculty regarding their opinion before making a decision.

Another perception of the effectiveness of the faculty senate focuses on its membership. As opposed to a representative form of governance where elected faculty represent their respective departments at the institution, Weingartner (1996) suggested that an environment where all faculty participate in the governance process would be more effective. This governance body also would include constituents from other groups on campus, such as administrators and exempt and nonexempt staff. Additionally, this version of a comprehensive electorate may or may not allow for more credibility, as individual representatives whose decisions may be tainted by personal and administrative views would not represent the faculty. To ensure that this body works, all "working" (p. 26) committees, or committees that are significant in the institutions functioning would be subordinate to the comprehensive senate to prevent it from merely being a discussion group (Weingartner, 1996).

THE FUTURE OF COMMUNITY COLLEGE SENATES

How decisions are made in community colleges has received an increased amount of discussion over the last decade, particularly as the community college has emerged as an area of study. Most of this research has emphasized the significance of the process recognizing the voice of the faculty on these campuses, specifically through faculty senates. Despite the successes of faculty senates, there are internal and external dynamics that will greatly impact the future of these types of organizations.

As faculty members in community colleges age and advance toward retirement, the opportunity to diversify the faculty with new hires is possible. The country, as well as the community college, continues to witness shifts in its demographics, with minorities, particularly Hispanics, becoming more visible in every aspect of the citizenry. Faculty members must collectively support the diversification of their ranks to ensure that these groups are represented. The diversification of the faculty provides positive role models for all students, while also promoting multiculturalism in other aspects of the campus, including the curriculum. Faculty senates must address this transformation and promote the hiring of more minorities within their ranks on their campuses.

Another trend that has been identified as older faculty members leave community colleges has been the increased dependence on part-time or adjunct faculty members. This number has increased from 22% of all faculty appointments in 1970 to more than 40% in 1993 (U. S. Department of Education, 1996). As this number increases, there are many consequences, including a lack of collegiality due to the transitional state of part-time faculty and also a deterioration of the faculty power base. Faculty senates are presently confronted with participation issues, but with the arrival of part-time faculty, this becomes even more of a problem. Part-time faculty are not allowed to participate in the governance process on many campuses due to constitutional restraints. Additionally, these individuals do not have the same concerns as full-time faculty, thus creating a fractionalization within the ranks. Therefore, faculty senates must be vocal in the establishment of statements regarding part-time faculty members to the administration who view the practice of hiring adjunct faculty as cost efficient and a short-term answer to the increase in the number of students entering community colleges.

In many parts of the county, faculty senates have to deal with powerful faculty unions. These organizations, as faculty senates, strive to prevent the erosion of faculty rights. However, as collective bargaining becomes more prevalent in other areas of the country, faculty senates must define a relationship with unions. As unions attempt to move on campuses, faculty senates become the last rationale for preventing unionization or the conduit through which faculty support for collective bargaining is garnered.

Privatization of services has become a major financial redeemer for many community colleges. By outsourcing, institutions gain a considerable amount of flexibility in their financial endeavors, while also gaining programs that are high quality and more comprehensive than the institution would have been able to provide, such as bookstores, food service, housing, and testing. Contrary to these benefits, there are some negative aspects. The most noteworthy downside would be a decrease in the amount of institutional control of the program or service. Beyond initial contract negotiations, faculty and administrators are sometimes removed from the decision-making process once privatization occurs. Consequently, faculty senates have less input regarding institutional operational issues. To prevent this, community college faculty senates must continue to have an active role in decision making regarding institutional financial matters.

Community college faculty senates may also be confronted with mission creep, a concept of institutional behavior where certain types of work assigned by a master plan become blurred or self-altered based on institutional leadership. The most common example is that of regional colleges trying to become research focused universities and community colleges wanting to award bachelors degrees. These arguments typically are initiated by institutional leadership and have anecdotally been a tool for college administrators to justify their own career progression. Faculty senates must become the institutional conscience to maintain a centered perspective on institutional mission. Senates can do this by working hard to maintain operational control of curriculum and faculty work-life issues.

With the increased emphasis on the role of faculty senates in community college governance, it is important for administrators, specifically presidents, to have knowledge of their roles, responsibilities, and rights. Professional associations such as the American Council on Education, the American Association of Community Colleges and American Association of Higher Education must be instrumental in providing skill training in this area.

CONCLUSION

During their first hundred years of existence, community colleges have established their missions based on providing vocational and transfer education to a diverse clientele with distinct characteristics and needs. As they enter the new millennium, they are going to continue to be confronted with many new challenges. Faculty senates will play a significant part in the efforts of these institutions to reinvent themselves.

Faculty serve as front-line workers in community colleges, and thus, it is important that they have an opportunity to participate in the development and enforcement of policy and strategic operations within these institutions. Even though the involvement of faculty in governance may sometimes be problematic, the inclusion of this group in decision making is important in producing greater variety and accuracy in outcome decisions. Additionally, broad-based decision making is important in gaining consensus and allowing faculty to feel a sense of ownership in institutional strategic planning and decision making.

The research focusing on community college faculty governance has been important in providing a picture of the process within these unique institutions. However, as the community college continues to evolve, the continued addition to the research in this area is essential. Furthermore, continued understanding and appreciation of faculty governance units by administrators is critical.

REFERENCES

American Association of Community and Junior Colleges. (1988). *Building communities: A vision for a new century. A report of the Commission on the Future of Community Colleges*. Washington, DC: National Center for Higher Education.

Armstrong, P., Miller, M. T., & Newman, R. (2001). *The community college faculty senate: Current trends and issues*. Unpublished manuscript, Jefferson State Community College, Birmingham, AL.

Baldridge, J. V. (1971). *Power and conflict in the university: Research in the sociology of complex organizations*. New York: John Wiley & Sons.

Bell, S. (1992). Research activities and work satisfaction of community college faculty. *The Review of Higher Education, 15*, 307-325.

Bergen Community College. (n.d.). Retrieved September 14, 2001, from http://www.bergen.cc.nj.us/.

Bergmann, B. (1991). Bloated administration, blighted campuses. *Academe, 68*(1), 12-16.

Boyer, E. L. (1990). *Scholarship reconsidered: Priorities of the professoriate*. San Francisco: Jossey-Bass.

Brint, S., & Karabel, J. (1989). *The diverted dream: Community colleges and the promise of educational reform, 1900-1985*. New York: Oxford University.

Broward Community College. (n.d.). Retrieved September 14, 2001, from http://www.broward.cc.fl.us/senate/.

Capital Community College. (n.d.). Retrieved September 14, 2001, from http://ccc.commnet.edu/libroot/senate/bylaws.htm.

Carlisle, B. A., & Miller, M. (1999). Current trends and issues in the practice of faculty involvement in governance. *Educational Review, 105*(5), 81-88.

Carnegie Foundation for the Advancement of Teaching. (1982). *The control of campus*. Washington, DC: Author.

Central Oregon Community College. (n.d.). Retrieved September 14, 2001, from http://www.cocc.edu/forum/constitution/constitution.htm.

Clark, B. R. (1970). The new university. In C. E. Kruytbosch & S. L. Messinger (Eds.), *The state of the university* (pp. 17-26). Beverly Hills, CA: Sage Publications.

Cohen, A. M., & Brawer, F. B. (1977). *The two-year college instructor today*. New York: Praeger.

Cohen, A. M., & Brawer, F. B. (1996). *The American community college* (3rd ed.). San Francisco: Jossey-Bass.

Colgan, C. (2001, September 15). *Freedom Paper No. 5: Administering higher education in a democratic society*. U.S. Department of State's Office of International Information Programs, http://usinfo.state.gov/products/pubs/freedom/freedom5.htm.

Cybert, R. M. (1979). Governance and administration of the university. In F. W. Bolman & C. C. Walton (Eds.), *Disorders in higher education* (pp. 90-117). Englewood Cliffs, NJ: Prentice Hall,

Daytona Beach Community College. (n.d.). Retrieved September 14, 2001, from http://faculty.dbcc.cc.fl.us/senate/FS%20Bylaws.htm.

Duke, R. G. (1997). Both sides now: Perspectives on community on community college workforce development. *The Catalyst, 24*(3), 11-15.

Evans, J. P. (1999). Benefits and barriers to shared governance in higher education. In M. Miller (Ed.), *Responsive academic decision-making: Involving faculty in higher education governance*. Stillwater, OK: New Forums Press.

Floyd, C. E. (1985). *Faculty participation in decision-making: Necessity or luxury*. Washington, DC: ASHE-ERIC Higher Education Report 8.

Gahn, S,. & Twombly, S. B. (1998, November). *Dimensions of the community college faculty labor market*. Paper presented at the Association for the Study of Higher Education Conference, Miami, FL.

Garavalia, B., Miller, M., & Miles, A. (1999, April). *Trends and issues of a community college: Jefferson State Community College, 1987-1997*. Annual meeting of the Council for the Study of Community Colleges, Nashville, TN.

Gilmour, J. E. (1991). Participative governance bodies in higher education: Report of a national study. In R. Birnbaum (Ed.), *Faculty in governance: The role of senate and joint committees in academic decision-making, New Directions for Higher Education Report 75* (pp. 27-40). San Francisco: Jossey-Bass.

Glendale Community College. (n.d.). Retrieved September 14, 2001, from http://www.gc.maricopa.edu/senate/SenateConstitution.html.

Hawthorne, E. M. (1991). Anticipating the new generation of community college faculty members. *Journal of College Science Teachers*, 365-368.

Hilosky, A., & Watwood, B. (1997, February). *Transformational leadership in a changing world: A survival guide for new chairs and deans.* Paper presented at the Annual International Conference of the Chair Academy, Reno, NV. (ERIC Document Reproduction System No. ED 407 027).

Hood, J. A. (1997). *An analysis of selection criteria, roles, skills, challenges and strategies of 2-year college presidents.* Unpublished doctoral dissertation, The University of Alabama, Tuscaloosa.

Kang, B., Newman, R. E., & Miller, M. T. (1998). Communication apprehension and role tendencies of faculty governance leaders. *Baylor Educator, 22*(3), 30-35.

Katsinas, S. (1996). Service is the key: Reflections on community college education. *Council on Universities and Colleges Newsletter, 5*(2), 6-14.

Keller, G. (1983). Academic strategy: The management revolution in American higher education. Baltimore: Johns Hopkins University.

Kerr, C. (1991). The great transformation in higher education. Albany: State University of New York.

Laab, T. R. (1987). Community college tenure: Teach or research? *Community/Junior College Quarterly, 11*, 267-273.

Mason, H. L. (1982). Four issues in contemporary campus governance. *Academe, 68*(1), 3A-14A.

Massachusetts Community College. (n.d.). Retrieved September 14, 2001, from http://www.tiac.net/users/mccc/.

Miles, A. S. (1987). *College law.* Tuscaloosa, AL: Sevgo.

Miles, A. S., Miller, M. T., & Anderson, L. A. (1996). Legal perspectives on faculty involvement in governance. In A. S. Miles (Ed.), *Legal liability issues for counselors in Alabama* (pp. 84-90). Livingston, AL: Alabama Counseling Association.

Miles, R. E. (1965). Human relations or human resources? *Harvard Business Review, 43*(4), 148-155.

Miller, M. T., McCormack, T. F., & Garavalia, B. J. (1997). Community college faculty involvement in governance: Implications for teaching. *Michigan Community College Journal, 3*(1), 51-61.

Miller, M. T. & Seagren, A. T. (1993). Faculty leader perceptions of improving participation in higher education governance. *College Student Journal, 27*, 112-118.

Miller, M. T., Vacik, S. M., & Benton, C. (1998). Community college faculty involvement in institutional governance. *Community College Journal of Research and Practice, 22*, 645-654.

Murphy. P. J. (1991). A collaborative approach to professional development. *Education Research and Perspectives, 18*, 59-65.

National Center for Education Statistics. (1994). *1994 digest of education statistics.* Washington, DC: U. S. Department of Education.

National Center for Education Statistics. (1997). *1997 digest of education statistics.* Washington, DC: U. S. Department of Education.

Palmer, J. C. (1992). The scholarly activities of community college faculty: Findings of a national survey. In J. C. Palmer & G. B. Vaughan (Eds.), *Fostering a climate for faculty scholarship at community colleges* (pp. 49-65). Washington, DC: American Association of Community and Junior Colleges.

Phelan, D. (1996, February). *Delegation and other team building processes: Transforming your department and programs.* Paper presented at the Annual International Conference of the National Community College Chair Academy, Phoenix, AZ. (ERIC Document Reproduction Service No. ED 394 557)

Pope, M. L., & Miller, M. T. (2000a). The skills and tasks associated with faculty leadership in community college governance. *Journal of Applied Research in the Community College, 7*(1), 5-12.

Pope, M. L., & Miller, M. T. (2000b). Community college faculty governance leaders: Results of a national survey. *Community College Journal of Research and Practice, 24*, 627-638.

Rifkin, T. (1997). *The profession and the person: Occupational and individual dimensions of community college faculty professionalism.* Dissertation Abstracts International. University Microfilms No. 9803962.

Rifkin, T. (1998). Differences between the PROFESSIONAL attitudes of full-time and part-time faculty. 10/05/01, ERIC, http://ericae.net/ericdb/ED417783.htm.

Salt Lake Community College. (n.d.). Retrieved September 14, 2001, from http://ecampus.slcc.edu/senate/index.html.

Schuster, J. (1991). Policing governance. *Academe, 77*(6), 33-36.

Seminole Community College. (n.d.). Retrieved September 14, 2001, from http://www.seminole.cc.fl.us/facultysenate/bylaws.htm.

Sergiovanni, T. J., & Starratt, R. J. (1988). *Supervision: Human perspectives* (4th ed.). New York: McGraw-Hill.

Sorrentio, S. A., & Hines, E. R. (1994). Community colleges and universities as providers of education and training. *Community College Journal of Research and Practice, 8*(5), 473-483.

Suffolk Community College. (n.d.). Retrieved September 14, 2001, from http://www.fascc.org/constitution.shtml.

Tidewater Community College. (n.d.). Retrieved September 14, 2001, from http://www.tc.cc.va.us/gov/facsen/docs/constit.htm.

U. S. Department of Education/National Center for Education Statistics. (1996). *Fall staff in postsecondary institutions.* Washington, DC: Author.

Valencia Community College (n.d.). Retrieved September 14, 2001, from http://faculty.valencia.cc.fl.us/association.

Vaughan, G. B. (1988). Scholarship in community colleges: Path to respect. *Educational Record, 69*(2), 217-237.

Vaughan, G. B. (1992). The community college unbound. In B. W. Dziech & W. R. Vilter (Eds.), *Prisoners of elitism: The community college's struggle for stature, New Directions for Community Colleges 78* (pp. 3-34). San Francisco: Jossey-Bass.

Weingartner, R. H. (1996). *Fitting form to function: A primer on the organization of academic institutions.* Phoenix, AZ: Oryx Press.

Williams, D., Gore, W., Broches, C., & Lostoski, C. (1987). One faculty's perceptions of its governance role. *Journal of Higher Education, 58*(6), 629-657.

CHAPTER 10

INVOLVING
FACULTY MEMBERS IN
INSTITUTIONAL FUNDRAISING

Thomas A. Bila
Bila, Graham, and Associates

During the past two decades, colleges and universities as well as many not-for-profits have come to rely greatly on fundraising efforts to replace or augment existing sources of revenue. In many instances, state appropriations have been reduced or have been static in growth, while in private institutions dramatic tuition increases have not been able to adequately combat rising operational costs. In both instances, reliance on fundraising activities and on endowment income has been transformed from providing a "margin of excellence" (Hoeflich, 1987), to providing a means of survival. The result has been increased amounts of money raised by higher education institutions as well as a greater institutional attention to the mechanisms for raising this money (Smith, 1996).

Market research for higher education fundraising has been inclusive in relating giving to undergraduate experiences, demographic trends, personality characteristics, giving ability, and frequently, the process of soliciting contributions (Bila, 1992; Connoly & Blanchette, 1986). Research into effective fundraising has even centered on faculty as donors, revealing that faculty provide financial contributions based on their positive

Policy and University Faculty Governance, 137–152

feelings toward their employing institution (Holland, Ritvo, & Kovner, 1997).

The process of raising money, as alluded to by the growing body of literature, is a complex process based jointly on donor motivation, communication, belief in the cause or case, and the process in which these are combined to form a solicitation (Rowland, 1986). This process of solicitation typically takes the form of a professional fundraising executive, such as a "development officer," but has more typically employed entire divisions for fundraising, ranging from professionals dedicated to donor research, annual gifts, major gifts, deferred gifts, capital campaigns, stewardship, alumni and cultivation activities, and record keeping.

To guide how faculty become involved in this process of raising institutional money, several fundamental terms related to fundraising activities need to be defined:

- *Annual Giving:*   an amount of money or service given annually; a fundraising program that generates gift support on an annual basis. Typically, these are a multitude of $25 and $50 gifts that are spent on immediate institutional needs.
- *Capital Campaigns:*   an intensive fundraising effort to meet a specific goal within a specified period of time for one or more major projects that are out of the ordinary, such as the purchase of equipment, or the acquisition of endowment funds. Although increasingly common, these multiyear campaigns usually are conducted every 7 or 10 years, and require a substantial institutional commitment.
- *Major Gifts:*   a significant contribution, dependent on the size, scope, and expectations for an institution. Many institutions will consider a gift in the $25,000 range "major"; however, some large and prestigious private institutions will consider "major" gifts only those in the six figure range.
- *Planned Giving:*   a systematic effort to identify and cultivate a person for the purpose of generating a major gift that is structured and that integrates sound personal, financial, and estate-planning concepts with the prospect's plans for lifetime or testamentary giving. A planned gift has tax implications and is often transmitted through a legal instrument, such as a will or a trust (Levy & Cherry, 1996).

These gift types have traditionally been conceptualized in a pyramid structure that defines a base of support as annual gifts (see Appendix). The pyramid concept holds that annual gifts and activities, such as volunteering for homecoming events or hosting athletic receptions are the entry point for future major donors. The role of the development officer then is to utilize a combination of marketing, research, communication, and personal investment strategies to move the entry-level donor to more substantial (higher gift) levels.

Although some may argue that involvement of faculty in fundraising should be treated as an issue separate from governance, there must be consideration given to the concept that fundraising is broadly revenue generation. The generation of this income often allows institutions to pursue agendas of promise or interest, and in this pursuit, institutions create a niche or unique market and notoriety for themselves. In a sense, the obtaining of financial resources has everything to do with institutional governance.

WHO RAISES MONEY?

Work in alumni and development relations necessitates a significant commitment of time in building relationships and trust between the institution and the alumni and friends of the institution. Unless the development and alumni officers have been part of the institution for some time (either as employees or as students and now alumni), they need the support and assistance of a strong board of trustees, a strong president, and a loyal faculty and staff. Although this seems expected, some institutions do not actively seek to involve the faculty, staff, administration, and board of trustees in all development and alumni activities, and consider the process an informal, family-type activity rather than a multibillion dollar industry.

Nearly two generations ago, the increase in fundraising campaigns as well as the increase in the number of development officers at colleges and universities was noted in the *Greenbrier Report:*

> In the years since the Second World War, a new administrative area in higher education has emerged. It is an area which does not even have a commonly understood name, as yet; it is sometimes called university (or college) relations, and sometimes a man rather than a job is given a title and simply called assistant to the president.... The precise dimensions of this area also lack definition. Some of its components are clear at first glance however; it obviously includes public relations, alumni relations, and fundraising. (1967, p. 31)

Research has indicated that to be successful and to assist in the long-term advancement of the institution, an alumni relations or development officer must remain at the institution for a minimum of three years (Bailey, 1988); however, development officers frequently leave before this three-year stay is completed (Bila, 1992). Bailey indicated that it takes this long to adequately determine institutional needs, to analyze the mission, to state the institutional case, and to win friends and contributions for the institution. Research continues to demonstrate (Panas, 1988) that the average development director (who is not part of senior management) remains at an institution for less than three years and then moves to another location, either by choice or by the request of senior-level administrators.

Some studies have shown that frequently the only way a development professional may get a significant increase in salary is to change employers, much the same as has been occurring with other professions in the United States (Bila, 2001a, 2001b; Duronio & Tempel, 1996, p. 16). A recent phenomenon has also come to play. Facing financial problems, there have been times that boards of directors and administrators who need to cut expenses end up cutting the budget of the development or alumni affairs offices, some of the few areas whose purpose is solely to increase philanthropic support. Even worse, in a cost-saving effort, some colleges and more than a few not-for-profits have shut down their development programs or closed their foundations. Perhaps because the development officers and alumni affairs directors have made their jobs *look* so easy, the college board members and/or administrators believe that the contributions will continue to arrive and there is no need for additional cultivation. Within two years they are in shock that their level of gifts has plummeted so greatly. Unfortunately, such short sightedness on the part of administration or board members has become far more common than one would expect.

In another vein, literature and professional programs have suggested that many alumni and development officers remain at an institution for a short period of time due to employer or institutional expectations which are unrealistic. Heuerman and Spitaels-Ginser (1985) suggested that professional organizations such as the NSFRE [now called AFP or the Association of Fundraising Professionals] and the Association for Healthcare Philanthropy (AHP) must stress to employers that:

1. Development and alumni relations are long-term/long-range projects and it is in the best interest of the institution to have a stable lengthy relation with the development/alumni officers;

2. Fundraising goals must be set based on the needs and setting of each institution—one institution's miracles may be another's bane; and

3. Development and alumni officers each have different areas of expertise and different sources of funding, so it is important to choose the one who can best address and relate to the sources of funding in the community (p. 10).

A common concern among higher education development officers is how to involve faculty in the identification, cultivation and eventual solicitation of alumni and friends of the institution, and how to use their expertise in building relationships between their former students and the institution. In addition to successfully collaborating with faculty to raise institutional support, development administrators can play a key role in helping faculty renew acquaintances with previous favorite students and can assist in institutional growth through the utilization of faculty to "paint pictures" of academic quality and the future in specific disciplines. The involved faculty member provides the stamp of authenticity that often makes a major difference in giving.

Being able to interact with the faculty is also very helpful to the development officer. The officer is able to hear some of the stories about alumni that he can share with donors as well as being able to hear from the faculty members about the needs of the college/university. Faculty members are usually very willing to share their needs with an officer who is able to fulfill or satisfy those needs. The development officer is also able to review, rewrite and improve the case for support based on the input of faculty members.

Of all individuals on campus, in dealing with donors as well as alumni, faculty members can be the most influential. From their classes and frequent interactions with students, long-term relationships can be constructed or destroyed. From the faculty member's teaching abilities and skills, students are inspired, and these points of interaction provide the rich fabric necessary for development officers to weave together a story of institutional need and promise. This is typically referred to as the statement of need or case for support.

A corollary could be formed. If alumni when they were students felt or perceived that they had poorly trained or uncaring faculty members or faculty who did not meet their needs, it will be highly unlikely that any solicitation for a contribution or any plea for help from these alumni will ever be successful.

A BASIC FUNDRAISING PHILOSOPHY

To better frame how faculty can be and are effectively involved, several principles for fundraising must be addressed. These principles are based generally on the growing research into fundraising effectiveness, and specifically on the professional dialogue which has created a tightly focused body of professional associations. They may vary based on institution, but generally can be accepted as guiding principles to raising money.

Guiding Fundraising Principles

1. People give to people.
2. People want the "happy experiences" or good feelings that giving to others provides.
3. People want to help the institution meet its needs and strengthen its mission.
4. Partnerships between donors and institutions may be formed which seek to advance the institution.
5. Annual giving provides a beginning for solicitation for future capital campaigns and for future planned gifts.
6. Trust between the institution and the donor is developed through proper institutional stewardship of gifts and time that is spent with each individual.
7. Most donors anticipate and expect recognition for their gifts.
8. Involving donors in developing a case statement for support is an easy way of soliciting their future financial support.
9. In any type of fundraising campaign, the rule of thumb is: 90% of the total amount of money raised will come from about 10% of the total number of donors who gave to that cause.
10. Donors give to an institution based on their own needs or interests, and not those that are stated or requested by the institution.

PRINCIPLES IN ACTION

People Give to People

Of all of the principles of fundraising that exist, perhaps the best known and most frequently stated is that people give to people. This concept refers to both the actual asking for the gift and the entire cultivation process of preparing a donor for a future gift.

There is no better principle to emphasize the importance of involving faculty members in any and all cultivation and solicitation efforts. Who better than faculty members to "rekindle" the positive feelings that alumni carry of their favorite professors or classes? These beloved professors can also reinforce the concept that alumni "owe" much of what they are today to the college and the faculty members who inspired them.

No matter how long the development or the alumni officer has been on campus, no matter how long a tenure the president has held, in each case, as a student, the alumnus/a had the most daily contact during the college years with faculty members.

No one else is as able to express passionately or forcefully the needs of a particular department or course of study as well as faculty members, for the faculty must use the equipment, teach and daily live with the state of their academic disciplines. These faculty members best "paint the picture" of what is needed, and from them, the donor is more likely to listen to the details of the needs or the case for support. Despite what some senior administrators may believe, especially those who have only been on campus for a relatively short period of time, most donors listen more to the view of their former faculty with whom they interacted in their youth.

People Want the Happy Experiences that Giving to Others Provide

In their *Seven Faces of Philanthropy,* Prince and File (1994) wrote that most donors have pleasant feelings when giving to an institution that they respect and admire. How is it that faculty and staff could assist in providing donors with these pleasant feelings? Again, the importance of the faculty members' ability to paint a picture or create a vision of what and how potential gifts benefit an institution must be stressed.

The simple thank you of faculty members that can be sent to donors can be a tremendous source of assistance to an institution. This thank you can greatly increase the level of good and pleasant feelings that have been generated from making a gift.

Often, faculty and even board members are frightened or uncomfortable with asking for a contribution. One easy way of providing them with some self-confidence as well as getting them used to being able to solicit a gift is to utilize their talents in making personal telephone calls to thank donors for their gifts.

In completing these thank-you telephone calls, it has been observed that more often than not, the donors may at first be a little apprehensive about the call. They may be expecting another solicitation for a gift. They are frequently and pleasantly surprised to hear another person expressing gratitude for the gift, especially if it is a faculty member who was liked and respected. Although research has yet to emphasize this tactic, empirical use, often discussed in professional associations, reinforces the positive influences of faculty assistance in expressing gratitude for financial contributions.

People Want to Help the Institution Meet its Needs

When alumni are proud of the college they graduated from, when they are proud of the degree that they hold, and when they feel that their education made them what they are today, they are willing to thank the institution either through volunteer work or through a financial contribution.

Faculty members are most able to assist in defining the needs of the institution as well as in defining the mission of the college. Their perceptions of who the students are, where they have come from, and where they are going, are the most important to the development office. The faculty members are the ones who have instilled a sense of pride in the alumni when they were students, and they demonstrate the mission to alumni and current students. Frequently, it is the faculty and staff members' tenure or desire to remain at the college that influences alumni giving patterns. Lengthy stays at the institution represent satisfaction with the institution to many alumni and demonstrates a loyalty to the mission and needs of the college which encourages donor and alumni loyalty and contributions.

Partnerships Between Donors and Institutions May be Formed

Most frequently, donors appreciate the opportunity of forming a partnership with the institution, and donors enjoy feeling that they are part of a "winning team" or a project that will demonstrate success. By sharing in this success, the donors form a partnership and feel close to the institution.

Perhaps the most logical goal of the professional development officer in higher education is to involve faculty in the very beginning of any fundraising campaign. Faculty, too, will want to be part of the winning team, and will be able to assist in campaigns both in their preparation and after they have begun.

Relying on faculty and staff allows the development officer to view the campaign from a holistic vantage point. In gaining the input from faculty, the development officer may strategize or more effectively plan to improve the campaign, often by adjusting or enhancing the fundraising techniques that involve team players such as faculty.

Faculty members are excellent in providing additional names of individuals who would be interested in the particular campaign or in developing the specific case for support. They also prove themselves to be invaluable in stating the case for support and in assisting the development officers in refining and honing objectives for raising institutional support.

Annual Giving Provides a Beginning for Solicitation for the Future

Most fundraising professionals agree that all giving is arranged in a "donor pyramid." The purpose of the annual fund is to attract the interest of the donor and then to eventually involve the donor in a major or special gift project, followed by a gift to a capital campaign, followed by the pinnacle of all gifts, a planned gift (see Appendix).

This pyramid has been the standard for fundraising practices for at least the past two decades, and continues to influence the majority of development alumni officers. Once a donor has become an annual donor, that is, once the donor has begun to make a regular annual contribution and has formed an initial loyalty to the institution, it then becomes a matter of cultivation to try to increase this donor's gift and to provide additional mechanisms for providing gifts to the college.

Assuming that the donor is willing to allow some publicity for the gift, this again provides an opportunity to involve faculty in the campaign. If the donor of a major gift is willing to have a picture appear in a local newspaper, in an alumni newsletter, in a magazine or in a local television news broadcast, it proves even more effective to include a faculty member and student who benefit from the contribution. This again emphasizes the integrity of the gift, and sends the message that the contribution provides a means of enhancing the educational aspect of the collegiate experience rather than individual or administrative promotion.

Faculty involvement also provides a mechanism for the beginning of cultivation of faculty as potential donors. Although there are always stereotypes that faculty members do not have sufficient financial resources, many faculty members are extremely loyal to their employing institutions. Many faculty members who have a long tenure at the college or university have owned their house during all that time. Some bought stocks during their youth and have held them for some years. Both groups may find that the values of housing and stocks have greatly increased and that they now could be called wealthy having an estate easily over $300,000.

Development officers frequently overlook faculty members in developing cultivation programs, thinking that faculty are typically more loyal (in financial terms) to their alma mater rather than their employer. The principle of "if you don't ask, you don't get" holds particularly true for most faculty members. Many faculty may feel honored and pleased to arrange a "living" memorial to their academic disciplines, perhaps even named after themselves, which would greatly benefit future generations. Just as faculty members can identify potential donors through alumni databases, they also should be given the opportunity to identify themselves and their colleagues for a current gift or for cultivation for a future gift.

Trust Between the Institution and the Donor is Developed through Institutional Stewardship

Donors who restrict their gifts to a specific department or account are interested in knowing or being shown that the gift really did go to the area requested. The use of faculty to emphasize this receipt, either by a thank-you phone call or through informing the donor of the gift's use, does much in assisting the donor to realize that the original contribution has been wisely used. This also demonstrates that the donor has a large degree of control over the contribution and that involvement through giving can make a significant difference.

Even with contributions of unrestricted funds, it is wise to contact donors to inform them of how their gifts have been used. Donors appreciate this personal contact, and frequently will provide additional funding to a project by simply being informed of how their gift has been used, how certain areas or needs still exist and how additional gifts that will be received may be used in the future.

Most Donors Anticipate and Expect Recognition

Most donors do expect some type of recognition for their gifts. In this era of high competition for philanthropic dollars, it seems unusual that there exist some institutions which do not follow the guidelines of acknowledging a gift within 72 hours of receipt. Frequently, due to computer problems or a shortage of staff, the processing of gifts can be placed on "the back burner," and as a result, donors do not receive an acknowledgment on a timely basis.

Many donors will no longer contribute to an organization that has not acknowledged a gift on a timely basis. As would be expected, the donor perceives that the organization does not need his/her gift since they failed to quickly respond or thank him/her for the gift. Another way in which a donor might perceive that his/her gift is not needed or appreciated is if the check that was sent is not cashed quickly. If the check is not deposited until after a few months have passed, it demonstrates to the donor that the money was not really needed.

Unless the donor requests anonymity, it is helpful to thank donors as frequently as possible, without adding huge expenditures to the budget. An annual report, as well as a quarterly honor roll of donors are always helpful in recognizing donors' generosity and loyalty.

The development office and the administration should determine an amount of a gift in which additional recognition or thanks would be helpful. Naturally, for a minimal contribution, three or four acknowledgements and a moderate premium would not be cost effective, nor would it be helpful to win future support. However, for more sizable gifts, recognition of this nature coupled with a letter of gratitude from a department chair or faculty member would be most appropriate. Involving the department chair or faculty member in this instance may indeed prove to be more meaningful than from a dean or senior-level administrator, as the faculty recognition demonstrates the power of a contribution at the grass-roots level.

Including faculty members in this acknowledgment process is extremely helpful. Their adding a thank you for a gift to their department or a scholarship fund or their simply writing a "P.S." on a standard acknowledgment letter will do much in encouraging the donor to make future gifts. A phone call, simply to say thank you, also would do much in making the donor feel and realize that the financial aid is truly needed and appreciated by all. This telephone call of acknowledgment is also an excellent teaching and training technique to assist faculty members in overcoming reluctance or apprehension about personally dealing with a contribution, perhaps even laying the ground work for the faculty member to solicit funds. Thanking a donor for a previous gift and not having to ask for a gift is fairly easy for most individuals. Also, it is a way to relax the caller and acclimate the faculty member in talking about specific dollar amounts, the power of these contributions, and developing an understanding about the procedures and processes used by the institution for fundraising.

Involving Donors in Developing a Case Statement is Vital to the Future

Many development officers conduct a study or a test to determine if the case for support that they have developed will be successful in attracting additional gifts to the college. The case for support is the central theme of any fundraising campaign, and as a result, it is crucial that as much input as possible is brought into the preparation of the case statement. All too often, development officers rely solely on communication with senior institutional administrators, and neglect the input of instructional and research faculty who have primary responsibility for program quality. The trend in recent years has been token involvement, utilizing nonspecific mailings to faculty asking for their indirect input into "things" that the college or university may "need."

Faculty at the institution will be the most helpful in determining the validity of the request for support, especially if they are willing to financially support it with their own resources. With faculty input, the case may be rewritten several times, until consensus is reached among faculty, academic and academic-support administrators, and development personnel. The intent is to create a vision for the institution which reflects a holistic approach to quality education and a vision which will elicit support from institutional alumni and friends.

Faculty as frontline employees, may be able to recall specific instances where students were unable to complete assignments or obtain adequate resources for lack of something specific, such as scholarship, computer technology, study areas, library facilities and resources, and so forth. That reference or recollection would assist in writing the story or the case, or in presenting that material the other alumni or potential donors. The more input that can be obtained, the better the case for support or the need statement becomes.

Ninety Percent of the Total Money Raised in a Particular Campaign or Cause Comes from Ten Percent of the Donors who Give to that Cause

Despite all of the work that is done to involve all of the donors or all of the alumni in making contributions to the college or university, the principle or tenet that has to be remembered is the "90/10" rule; 90% of the entire amount of money raised for the particular need comes from 10% of the donors.

What has become somewhat startling to all development professionals who have been in fundraising for at least the past 25 years or so is that when they began their careers, the ratio was 80/20 or 80% of the entire amount of money raised came from 20% of the total number of people who contributed to that campaign. If the trend continues that began in some major campaigns in the late 1990s, the new rule of thumb soon will be 95/5 or 95% of the total raised will be coming from only 5% of the total donors who give to this case.

Usually, the president, board of trustees, and the development officers will deal with the 10% of the wealthy or most generous donors. However, to demonstrate a unified campus as well as assisting the campus community to feel a sense of accomplishment, it will be necessary to include and work with all donors, whether they are major donors or not. Including faculty and staff members in work with "minor" donors (those who are not able to contribute a gift in the six figure range, or whatever institutional formula or criteria is used to describe a major donor) is a way of allowing all donors to feel a sense of worth and importance to the institution. Also, it provides the faculty with the opportunity of maintaining contacts with some of their more favorite former students or the more illustrious alumni.

Faculty members looking for assistance with their classes, as far as external speakers to validate what they are teaching, would be assisted by this particular opportunity to network with the graduates of their institution. Frequently, students need this type of outside or external stimulus (having a successful alumnus/a returning to the class to talk to students) to be more conscientious as to their studies and to assist them in determining their future career goals.

Donors Give to an Institution Based on their Own Needs or Interests

Again, although this would seem to be a very common-sense statement that anyone would understand and grasp and that all would agree with, yet, a number of capital and annual campaigns are established using cases for support that are far too glamorous to encourage a donor to become a participant in the campaign. Cases for support to repair the plumbing fixtures, to comply with the Americans with Disabilities Act, to lay new sewers, and to build parking lots are just a few examples of the lack of foresight or thought that some administrations place in their planning process.

There is even a case at a college where I worked as a consultant in which the new president wanted to destroy an unused old building on campus, replace it with a parking lot, and cover the current parking lot with an educational excellence center. The motivation for this construction: a demonstration to the community that the college was focused on progress and the arts. As the institution was focused on middle-class students who would be the first in their families to graduate from college, this case was not easily (nor eventually) planned in light of the institution's capabilities or need. The new president, however, believed that he could change the vision of the college early in his tenure, and had no concept that the college, faculty, and key alumni would end up in turmoil over his grand ideas. I attributed this lack of knowledge to his lack of experience at being a president, since this was the first time he had this full-time responsibility.

The key to planning effective fundraising is to garner alumni and potential donor support, and develop consensus on campus between those constituents and campus constituents, particularly faculty and students. Faculty members, if they are indeed responsible for institutional prestige (through research, teaching, service and preparing future alumni), must be involved in communicating with the potential donors to find a common set of needs. In this scenario, the development office becomes a fulcrum in which different power centers are brought to collaboration.

INVOLVING FACULTY IN DEVELOPMENT

Faculty members need to be involved in the fundraising process. This is true as the dollars raised will usually most influence the faculty, either through scholarships that are offered to attract better or more qualified students, or through improvements that are for the betterment of their departments.

Some development officers may claim that there are some negatives associated with including faculty in the identification and solicitation of donors. They feel that faculty may unduly influence donors so that they are able to obtain items that they personally want, or are able to influence donors to support their individual cases for support. Many development office personnel also claim that faculty are slow to respond, lack organization to follow in garnering involvement, and place individual needs above institutional needs. Perhaps with more communication and work with the faculty members, the development staff will recognize their value and appreciate their commitment to serve.

Many institutions also follow the custom of having students who are receiving scholarships or financial aid write to donors to thank them for the financial assistance. Most frequently, the development office will monitor the letter writing to first make sure that it is grammatically correct and to make certain the student or recipient does not ask the donor for additional financial assistance after college, or for other nonacademic needs.

Although there are some gauges or tests that exist that can be used to identify the best individuals to solicit potential donors for contributions, frequently it will be necessary for the development officers to identify the best faculty members for involvement. Some may volunteer who actually will prove to be a detriment to the college and its programs. The most common form of soliciting faculty involvement is through traditional governance mechanisms, such as asking a college dean for faculty members who might be involved. This top-down identification, however, may often prove to be both discouraging for faculty who recognize the power of involvement in fundraising, and frustrating for those working to establish clear lines of faculty involvement through a senate or similar forum.

Faculty can play an important role in institutional fundraising, but this role is one that must be bartered among faculty and administrative groups. There are real benefits to involving faculty in fundraising, and faculty must learn to accept this type of behavior if they intend to benefit from it. Current barriers concerning the involvement of faculty in resource allocation tend to be perceptual—on both the part of faculty who may resent being asked to do this and administrators who may see faculty unfit for this type of service. Efforts to maximize institutional effectiveness, then, must be educational in nature to begin with, but must also be visionary and mutually beneficial.

APPENDIX

Pyramid Concept of Academic Alumni Giving

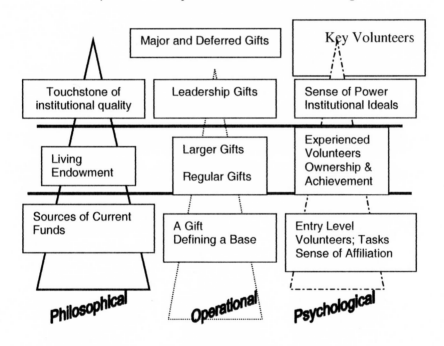

REFERENCES

Bailey, W. (1988). Turnover in hospital fund raising: Asking the tough questions. *Fund Raising Management, 3*, 90-91.

Bila, T. A. (1991). *Certified fund-raising executives: Their profile and the approaches they have used to obtain their current employment.* Unpublished doctoral dissertation, Southern Illinois University at Carbondale.

Bila, T. A. (1992, September). Planned gifts hold great promise. *Board Fundraising Strategies, 4*(3), 26.

Bila, T. A. (2001a). *The fundraising professional in Minnesota.* Minneapolis, MN: Association of Fundraising Professionals.

Bila, T. A. (2001b). *The fundraising professional in Eastern Iowa.* Minneapolis, MN: Association of Fundraising Professionals.

Connolly, M. S., & Blanchette, R. (1986). Understanding and predicting alumni giving behavior. In J. A. Dunn (Ed.), *Enhancing the management of fund raising* (pp. 69-89). San Francisco: Jossey-Bass.

Duronio, M. A., & Tempel, E. R. (1996). *Fund raisers: Their careers, stories, concerns and accomplishments.* San Francisco: Jossey-Bass.

Greenbrier Group. (1967). The Greenbrier report. *College and University Journal, 6*(1), 1-40.

Hoeflich, M. H. (1987). Prospects for college and university fund raising. *Academe, 73*(1), 30-32.

Holland, D., & Bean, J. (1990). *The strategic management of college enrollments.* San Francisco: Jossey-Bass.

Holland, T. P., Ritvo, R., & Kovner, R. (1997). *Improving board effectiveness* (1st ed.). American Hospital Association.

Huerman, J. N., & Spitaels-Genser, E. (1985, Summer). Mirror, mirror on the wall. *NAHD Journal,* 10-11.

Levy, B. R., & Cherry, R. L. (Eds.). (1996). *The NSFRE fund-raising dictionary.* New York: John Wiley & Sons.

Panas, J. (1988). *Born to raise.* Chicago: Pluribus Press.

Prince, R. A., & File, K. M. (1994). *The seven faces of philanthropy.* San Francisco: Jossey-Bass.

Rowland, A. W. (Ed.). (1986). *Handbook of institutional advancement* (2nd ed.). San Francisco: Jossey-Bass.

Smith, S. B. (1996). *Growth of foundation funding in doctoral university I and Ii during a period of decreasing state appropriations.* Paper presented at the Annual Meeting of the Association for the study of Higher Education, Memphis, TN.

CHAPTER 11

CONCLUSION

Defining a Critical Meaning for
Shared Governance

Michael T. Miller
University of Arkansas

Faculty involvement in governance is conceptually grounded in the idea of academic democracy, where a form of representation is utilized to express a will of the academic citizenry. The problems associated with representative democracy are many, ranging from the identification and following of mob mentalities to the manipulation of popular opinion and use of polling as an agenda setting device. The fundamental concern for college administrators, policy makers, and faculty members, though, is more basic and tied into how decisions are made and who can and should be involved in making those important decisions.

The body of literature related to institutional decision making is substantial, yet the management strategies expressed and advocated are often shallow and do not take root as long-term management strategies. Birnbaum (2000) noted and described this, identifying the idea of management "fads" in higher education, and the importance of tradition and institutional culture as being overwhelming barriers to changing institutional decision making. Rosovsky (1990) argued this artfully, and painted

Policy and University Faculty Governance, 153–159

a truthful picture of the academy that holds that change is gradual at best and that institutional culture defines all things. So from a practical standpoint, attempting to generalize the meaning, use, structure, and issues associated with faculty senates and similar governance units is inherently problematic. This is not insurmountable, however, and does not need to be addressed entirely in isolation from other institutions and settings.

As Rosser noted earlier in this text, the history of shared governance can be traced to forming roots of higher education. Yet, the tradition alluded to has never truly been the norm for American higher education (Baldridge, 1982), and as Davis pointed out, the push-and-pull relationship between trustees, administrators, and faculty is largely conflict driven. This parameter suggests something more than management strategies, as might be argued by Birnbaum, and clearly places the use and dependence on shared governance not on institutional culture but rather on the relationship and communication behavior of administrators and faculty. The Miller, Williams, and Garavalia chapter made an attempt to break down the communication patterns of faculty senate members during their formal shared governance meetings, but it is perhaps Bila's chapter on fund raising that provides the best case analysis of the relationship between faculty and administrators.

Bila outlined a premise for fund raising and the roles to be played by both administrators and faculty. He argued rather distinctly that academic planning and institutional self-understanding provide the causes to be addressed in fund raising activities, and provides the observation that faculty are the ideal stewards for defining an institutional plan, the tools to implement the plan, and the incentive for private donors to support the vision of the plan. The role of administrators becomes distinct as well, as they provide the necessary support, background, muscle, and foresight necessary to implement fund raising and marketing efforts. The entire process only works when both parties can define their roles, acknowledge these roles, and work to fulfill specific tasks. This observation by Bila is indeed the case of where faculty involvement successfully intersects with decision making to bring meaning, focus, and success to institutional efforts.

By accepting this notion of Bila's, faculty involvement in governance fails when role ambiguity prevails and there is a lack of acknowledgement of faculty or administrative actions. Additionally, the implementation of his argument would hold that recognition of inputs are important, and that the value of higher education from a philosophical perspective still has a great deal to do with the academic content of a college experience and that faculty involvement should be directed to this end.

While Bila's chapter may provide the clearest singular example of shared governance at work, each chapter does provide some basic addition to the critical conversation about how faculty are and should be involved in shared governance. For clarity, a few points from each chapter have been distilled into the following sections: issues for faculty, issues for administrators, and issues for collaboration.

Issues for Faculty

Within the domain of shared governance faculty play an important role, but a role that needs further definition and greater clarity. Caplow and Heinen's chapter provides good evidence that the role of the college faculty member is certainly ambiguous and often misunderstood. The lessons presented by these chapters indicates, though, that faculty members have a responsibility to define their actions and must learn to project what types of outcomes they expect. An attitude of being "allowed" to participate will often result in the status quo and institutional tradition will, by default, relegate faculty activities to a lowest common denominator. The tradition of faculty activism in the 1960s, however, provides the counter argument, yet does not get at the notion of responsibility.

The stand-off between faculty and administrators of the 1960s, and the 1990s according to Kors and Silverglate (1998) goes a great distance to demonstrate that faculty passion can inspire and motivate faculty to involvement. But, is this involvement responsive to the issues in need of faculty participation, and is the involvement responsible within the parameters of the decisions to be made? Often these are the questions that need to be addressed, but are overlooked in pursuit of the more glamorous issues of facility utilization and athletic planning. Indeed, even a cursory examination of the issues addressed by the contemporary faculty senate will probably result in the identification of tangential issues and agendas dictated by special interest groups and larger institutional concerns rather than the important faculty-driven conversations about curriculum and the intellectual life of the college student. The conversation about the installation of Starbucks seems to carry greater weight for the contemporary faculty senate than questions of general education reform.

Specific questions for faculty members to consider include:

- How can faculty members be educated about being responsive and responsible to institutional issues?
- What incentives might be successful to motivate the best and brightest faculty to participate in hard decision making that can consume large amounts of time and potentially impact, either positively or negatively, their academic careers?

- Which faculty leaders can inspire and motivate others to participate in a meaningful way at all levels of the university?
- What are the trends in faculty hiring, evaluation, and reward, and what kinds of impact do these trends have on garnering a new generation of involved faculty members?
- What kinds of faculty involvement have the greatest impact and residual campus impact on the process of sharing authority?

Issues for Administrators

Vacik and Borland hit on important ideas in their chapters related to the administrators responsibility for knowing and understanding positional roles and responsibilities in regard to faculty empowerment. The ideas expressed are certainly more than training a manager to respect a democratic workplace, and run deeply into academic administrator's beliefs about democracy as a moral imperative in education. The impact of a moral imperative intersects with basic ideas and institutional thinking about hiring and placing key administrative personnel based on their beliefs and willingness to engage faculty, and not just about administrative efficiency. Aronowitz (2000), among others, makes this claim forcefully and clearly spells out the need for those with a respect and passion for academic matters to pursue and be placed in administrative posts. Aronowitz noted that quite the opposite is happening, as business practices are placed decidedly in front of academic matters, and that a fluency in administrative efficiency can outpace intellectual rigor and ability in the current university.

Campbell (2000) took a slightly different approach to the same problem, arguing that special interest groups and trustees conspire to dictate the agenda of colleges and universities. This dictation places academic integrity near the bottom of institutional priorities and administrators more often than not fall prey to special interest group pressure. Examples of special admissions, waived requirements, inflated grades, and turning a deaf ear to curricular reform have been noted as responses to special interest group pressure. As Vacik, Davis, Bila, and even Pope point out in this text, administrative skills are increasingly important, but are only effective when framed within a context of respect and value for the academic component of the university.

Specific questions to be addressed by college administrators might include:

- What are the priorities of faculty involvement in governance? What are the priorities in academic and academic-support areas? In business operations?

- What domains should faculty be involved in and in what domains do faculty members have a right and expectation to be involved in?
- How should faculty be involved in areas that are exclusively academic support and carry long-term financial implications for the campus?
- What kinds of tools or measures can be used to indicate if faculty involvement is having a positive impact on any or all of the institution's behaviors and decisions?
- What are the barriers to stronger faculty involvement in institutional governance, and what specific actions can administrators take to build a more efficient and responsive system of shared governance?

Issues for Collaboration

The bridge for successful collaboration between faculty members and administrators is largely constructed on the idea of mutual trust, respect, and understanding. As suggested by Aronowitz, faculty have increasingly little respect for the academic integrity of administrators as they increasingly serve in a business-focused capacity. Administrators have increasingly little respect for faculty members, accusing them of living in ivory towers and producing seldom-read literature and obscure publications. The solution may be seen in developing institutional trust between faculty and administrators, and lends credence to the work of those such as McDonald (2002) who cite the extreme need to build campus community. For faculty and administrators, though, it is more than creating an initial linkage, and requires meaningful dialogue about important campus issues and visions. A "gypsy-administrator" workforce that is derived from external agencies and sources does not typically foster a collaborative environment, but the issue of trust and institutional devotion must be addressed from both sides. Faculty who spend entire careers at a single institution must be willing to explore new ideas and different approaches to problem solving, and administrators new to campus must be respectful of institutional culture and heritage.

The problem remains to some extent that the current generation of academic administrators are more concerned with work-flow systems, outsourcing, and financial issues than with the academic life of an institution. At the heart of this disparity is a basic question of the purpose and definition of higher education. As Karabell (1998) noted, the inefficiencies and ambiguity surrounding higher education and its traditions only serve to raise public scrutiny of the academy, and is only reflective of an increasingly public question about the role, function, and purpose of higher education. This question is well deserved on the public front as college costs have increased dramatically, but it is perhaps the most disheartening to find that this conversation is hardly echoed on the college campus, as concerns over outsourcing and contract management have subsumed the agenda of the leading academic officer on most campuses.

Some basic and important questions that might be addressed include:

- How can faculty members and administrators at all levels work more efficiently to produce a marriage of shared interests and mutual respect?
- How can the agendas of faculty and administrators be identified and shared to create an institutional agenda based on a common good rather than special interest group desires?
- What kinds of administrative and faculty behaviors serve as disincentives to shared governance? What can be done to change these behaviors to allow for greater collaboration?
- What kinds of discussions should consistently be considered "fair-game" in shared governance? What kinds of issues and topics should be off limits?

Future Agenda Items

Clearly, the university of the past is gone and business practices and influences are an accepted component of institutional life (Rojstaczer, 1999), but they need not be the overarching theme for the university in the twenty-first century. As noted in Miller's (1999) examination of shared faculty governance, the primary concern has to be related to the good of the institution and the good of higher learning. When those focusing statements get lost in debates over rights involvement, the entire notion of collaborative management becomes misconstrued.

The historical discussion presented here supports the tradition of shared governance, and Bai's observations on national issues of shared governance reinforce that the tradition of collegial shared governance will remain. This future must face a long list of challenges, including reward structures for involvement, levels of faculty empowerment, faculty leadership training, faculty responsiveness to issues and responsibility for decision making, and issues of equity in decision making and participation. On the part of administrators, questions of the legal rights of faculty to be involved prevail, as do issues of timely decision making, information sharing and communication of sensitive data, and the question of allowing or encouraging grassroots decision making for the welfare of the larger group.

The future of shared governance, then, must go back to the most basic questions about higher education as suggested by Rosser: what is the purpose of higher education and higher learning, what is the purpose of shared decision making, and how does it all fit together. The failure to synthesize philosophic questions with pragmatic daily issues will result in the continued trend of treating higher education like a for-profit business and the continued decline of meaningful academic conversations about issues such as the intent of general education or content of general studies courses. The future of shared decision making, as well as higher education, hangs in the balance of the current generation of faculty governance leaders and college administrators and the steps they choose to take or issues they choose to avoid during the next decade. Change is inevitable for the academy, but the distinct rituals, rights, and customs of the university have been waning rapidly during the past two decades, and unless faculty claim a responsible, responsive role in decision making, the university will forever be relegated to functioning more like a for-profit business than an instrument of social good.

REFERENCES

Aronowitz, S. (2000). *The knowledge factory dismantling the corporate university and creating true higher learning.* Boston: Beacon.

Baldridge, J. V. (1982). Shared governance: A fable about the lost magic kingdom. *Academe, 68*(1), 12-15.

Birnbaum, R. (2000). *Management fads in higher education: Where they come from, what they do, and why they fail.* San Francisco: Jossey-Bass.

Campbell, J. R. (2000). *Dry rot in the ivory tower.* Lanham, MD: University Press of America.

Karabell, Z. (1998). *What's college for? The struggle to define American higher education.* New York: Basic.

Kors, A. C., & Silverglate, H. A. (1998). *The shadow university the betrayal of liberty on America's campuses.* New York: Harper Collins.

McDonald, W. M. (Ed.). (2002). *Creating campus community.* San Francisco: Jossey-Bass.

Miller, M. T. (Ed.). (1999). *Responsive academic decision making involving faculty in higher education governance.* Stillwater, OK: New Forums.

Rojstaczer, S. (1999). *Gone for good tales of university life after the golden age.* New York: Oxford University.

Rosovsky, H. (1990). *The university—an owner's manual.* New York: W. W. Norton.

ABOUT THE AUTHORS

Dr. Kang Bai is the Coordinator of Institutional Effectiveness and Research at Troy State University in Dothan, Alabama. Dr. Bai has published extensively in the area of faculty development assessment, particularly focusing on sabbatical leave programs. He was previously the Chair of the Department of English Language Instruction at Nanning University in China, and he is active in the Association for Institutional Research. (BKang@troyst.edu)

Dr. Thomas A. Bila is the Executive Director of the Minnesota Friends of the Orphans, and international organization dedicated to helping provide the children of Latin America and the Caribbean with food, clothing, shelter, medical care, and an education. Dr. Bila has previously served as the Vice President for Institutional Advancement at Western New England College and the Director of Major and Annual Gifts at Southern Illinois University. He is an active member of the National Society of Fund Raising Executives and publishes in the area of philanthropy and donor behavior. (tbila@friendsmn.org)

Dr. Kenneth W. Borland, Jr., has served as a faculty member and/or senior level academic administrator in three universities: Associate Professor of Higher Education at Dallas Baptist University, a private university with a limited Faculty Council and no collective bargaining or tenure tracks; Assistant Professor of Higher Education and Assistant Vice Provost for Academic Affairs at Montana State University, a Land Grant with a Faculty Council and no collective bargaining, and; Associate Provost at East Stroudsburg University of Pennsylvania where there is a strong faculty union presence in governance. He was awarded the Doctor of Education by the The Pennsylvania State University where he studied Adult and Higher Education. His teaching and research focus on undergraduate academics and academic leadership.

Dr. Julie Caplow is an Associate Professor in the School on Information Science and Learning Technology at the University of Missouri–Columbia. Dr. Caplow previously served as the Executive Director of the Association for the Study of Higher Education (ASHE) and as an Associate Professor in Educational Leadership and Policy Analysis at the University of Missouri. Her teaching and research interests have focued on postsecondary curriculum and instruction; specifically college teaching, faculty governance, problem-based learning, and educational technology in postsecondary instruction.

Houston D. Davis is the Assistant Vice President of Academic Affairs and the Assistant to the President at Austin Peay State University in Clarksville, Tennessee. Prior to this position, he served for four years on the staff of the Tennessee Higher Education Commission. He holds a PhD from Vanderbilt University in Nashville, Tennessee. (DAVISH@apsu.edu)

Dr. Brian J. Garavalia is currently affiliated with the University of Kansas conducting research in the areas of cultural anthropology, adult community development and behavior, and education. He has previously served on the faculty of Valdosta State University in Georgia and has worked in international affairs at Southern Illinois University at Carbondale.

Ethan Heinen is a doctoral student in Educational Policy at the University of Missouri–Colombia. For the past two years, he has worked with the Consortium for Educational Policy Analysis at the University of Missouri–Colombia conducting educational evaluations. His research interests include higher education and K-12 policy analysis, politics of education, gifted education, and school choice.

Dr. Michael T. Miller is an Associate Professor of Higher Education at the University of Arkansas. He was formerly the Associate Dean of the College of Education at San Jose State University and Professor of Higher Education. He served as the Director of the National Data Base on Faculty Improvement in Governance from 1994-1999 and was on the Higher Education program faculty at the University of Alabama. He was a faculty member in Adult and Vocational Education at the University of Nebraska, and is the author of *Academic Leadership in Community Colleges* and *Improving Faculty Governance Cultivating Leadership and Collaboration in Decision-making*.

Dr. Myron L. Pope is an Assistant Professor of Adult and Higher Education at the University of Oklahoma. Dr. Pope has also served as the Director of Student Recruitment for the College of Education at the University of Alabama and as the Talent Search Coordinator for Alabama Southern Community College. His research areas include faculty work as it relates to student access and issues of diversity on campus. (myronp@ou.edu)

Vicki J. Rosser is an assistant professor in the Department of Educational Leadership and Policy Analysis at the University of Missouri–Colombia. She is the coeditor of the book *Understanding the Work and Career Paths of Midlevel Administrators in Higher Education*. Her research interests include faculty and (midlevel) administrative worklife issues, academic leadership, and governance. Vicki's most recent work focuses on the leadership effectiveness of academic deans as evaluated by their college faculty and administrative staff members.

Dr. Steve Vacik is the Associate Dean of the Campus at Bevill State Community College in Fayette, Alabama. Dr. Vacik has responsibility for the daily operation of the campus, including faculty development and assessment. His research interests include history of American higher education and group dynamics. He also served as the Director of Student Support Services also at Bevill State Community College.

Dr. Carl Williams is the Director of Graduate School Recruitment at the University of Alabama where he also serves on the faculty of the Higher Education Administration Program. Dr. Williams' background is in political science and public administration, particularly focusing on the university as a political entity.